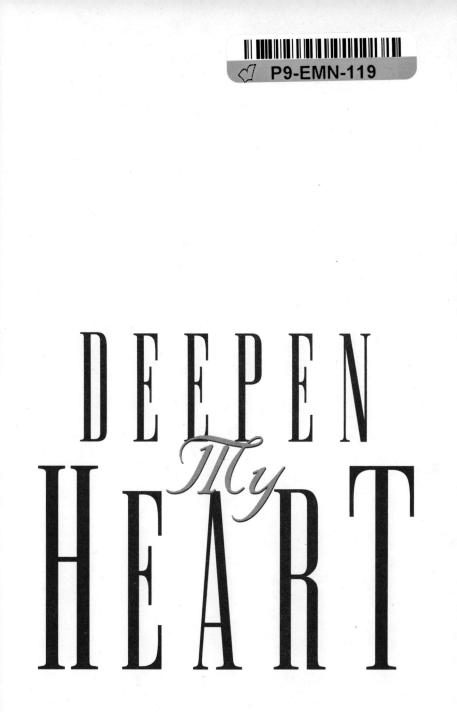

DEEPEN
My
HEART

STEVEN MOSLEY

DEEPEN *My* HEART

REVIEW AND HERALD® PUBLISHING ASSOCIATION
HAGERSTOWN, MD 21740

The author assumes full responsibility for the accuracy of all facts
and quotations as cited in this book.

Unless otherwise noted, Bible texts in this book are from the *Holy Bible, New
International Version.* Copyright © 1973, 1978, 1984, International Bible Society. Used by
permission of Zondervan Bible Publishers.

Scripture quotations marked NASB are from the *New American Standard Bible,* ©
The Lockman Foundation 1960, 1962, 1963, 1968, 1971, 1972, 1973, 1975, 1977.

This book was
Edited by Gerald Wheeler
Copyedited by William Cleveland and James Cavil
Interior design by Patricia S. Wegh
Cover design by GenesisDesign
Cover illustration by Matthew Pierce
Typeset: 11/14 Garamond Book Condensed

PRINTED IN U.S.A.

02 01 00 99 98   5 4 3 2 1

R&H Cataloging Service
Mosley, Stephen R., 1952-
     Deepen my heart.

     1. Spiritual life.   2. Christian life.
I. Title.

                    248.4

ISBN 0-8280-1285-7

Contents

Part One

The Need to Deepen Our Hearts

Chapter One

There's Got to Be More to It Than This

My Christian life is going nowhere. It's been like that for years."

Tad's voice seemed to bounce off the windshield and hit me in the face as we drove back from a church social. I didn't think I'd heard right. "Are you serious?"

He took a deep breath. "Steve, I've been waiting for something to happen for so long. Do you know what it's like to sit there in the pew and just . . . suffocate?"

Actually I did know what it was like to sit there and feel bored to tears. But this sounded a lot more serious. How could it be happening to Tad? He had the perfect family: a lovely, supportive wife who led a small Bible study group, and two beautiful children. I remembered his boy and girl standing shyly on the platform in the sanctuary, reciting a whole quarter's worth of memory verses, the only kids in their class who'd been able to do so.

Squeezing my hands on the steering wheel, I tried hard to think of something useful to say. The only thing that came out was "The sermons are that boring?"

"It's not just that. I'm tired of jumping through hoops and never feeling that I'm somewhere I haven't already been. A lot of times I just want to scream, 'Where in the world's the Holy Spirit?' I feel as if I've been doing it all on my own."

We were driving past the immaculate lawns of the upscale townhouses in our church's neighborhood—the same manicured scene I'd passed countless times with my family and with Tad's. We were fortunate to be able to worship in this tightly zoned piece of southern California paradise. I wondered why my friend couldn't just appreciate what he had.

"Is there some problem that's got you down?"

"No. No disasters. Linda and I and the kids are OK. I know I shouldn't complain. But . . ." Tad searched for words, his hands waving in the air, "there's *got* to be more to it than this."

Although I could sense the pent-up desperation in his voice, I still didn't want to believe it. There had to be more than what? What could be missing? I decided to reason with the man.

"Tad, you've been a great teacher in Bible classes and seem to have really enjoyed those small group sessions we had. You've got a great family. And you've got all kinds of talent. People love you—"

"And I'm dead," Tad interrupted. "I don't see God doing anything in this place. I'm going through the motions, but I never sense God moving in my life. Just once wouldn't it be nice to get off dead center?"

I looked out the window. It was a perfectly gorgeous day. The sun leaped out of a spotless azure sky, bathing our suburb in technicolor hues. But here Tad was sitting beside me talking about being dead. It didn't make sense. After all, what about his Easter banner?

Tad had a sharp, creative mind and was something of an artist. The congregation particularly appreciated the Easter pendant he'd made to hang over the baptistry. It showed Christ's pierced hands lifted up and silhouetted against bold rays of golden sunlight. Above those hands was the image of a dove springing into flight. I shook my head. It didn't seem possible that the creator of that dazzling statement could be stuck in a spiritual rut. But I was starting to feel extremely worried.

"Is there anything I can do, Tad?"

"No, it's not you—it's not anybody. It's me. If only I didn't feel that God was doing nothing—absolutely nothing—inside me. It's just so different from when I first became a Christian. The Bible was so alive then. All the sermons I heard seemed to come straight from heaven. God was right there . . . so close. But now . . . I can't go on like this. It's a farce."

Pulling up at Tad's house, I turned off the engine. We looked each other in the eye. He was being straight with me, and I wanted to be straight with him. But I felt pretty helpless. What could I say that might give him some hope? Somehow I made a few pathetic attempts at encouragement—I don't remember what I said exactly. We shook hands. After I gave him a pat on the shoulder, he strode up his driveway—and out of my life.

After that, when I'd call Tad for some tennis with the guys, he would always have an excuse. He and Linda didn't show up for Saturday night parties anymore. And his familiar spot at the church—left side, three pews from the front—is still empty.

We now sing our hymns about the glories of the Christian life, looking up at that glorious Easter banner and wondering what happened to the artist. Why didn't the Resurrection happen in his life? That green, gold, and white tapestry dramatically captures the supernatural moment Jesus rose from the dead—a broken human body transformed into an eternal Saviour. But now I realize that it was more a desperate plea than a statement of faith. It was a passionate cry to God that none of the rest of us heard. It's only in the aftermath that I begin to see how much Tad wanted someone to understand what he was going through.

I don't think Tad abandoned God. I believe he simply felt compelled to take his spiritual quest elsewhere. And I hope he finds "something more than this." But I am haunted by that empty place in the pew near where I sit. And one of the reasons is that my friend's malaise is not that different from my own. Now, much later, I realize that his anguished questions have become my own.

Tad was a bit more intense than the rest of us. A broad stripe of the melancholic artist ran through him. And so he had a lower tolerance for mediocrity of the spirit than most. He felt spiritual inertia more keenly.

But we've all tasted it. Almost all believers go through a period in their spiritual lives when nothing—absolutely nothing—seems to be going on. We usually can look back at the time of our conversion and see some fireworks. Sometimes we can point to some crisis that helped us rediscover God's presence. But now we endure long stretches of the doldrums. With no wind, no waves, the ship of faith sits deathly still in the water. And our prayers seem to wither in the suffocating atmosphere.

How do we deal with spiritual stagnation?

SECOND VERSE, SAME AS THE FIRST

It's hard to get excited about the good news when you've heard it all before. The Bible is so familiar. The cross is an old story. Church is the same old thing.

Sometimes we attempt to generate some wind in the sails on our own. Perhaps we look for help in the headlines, trying to get enthusiastic about some new catastrophe or conspiracy that surely points us toward the end-time. We hope the sensation of standing on the edge of a cliff will wake us up. But often this gets to be a rut as well, and we have to keep finding new catastrophes and conspiracies, surefire signs of an impending apocalypse. People turn into prophecy aficionados, endlessly plotting end-of-the-world scenarios.

Others of us try to generate momentum through doctrinal battles. We struggle to cut error away from the body of Christ. The unspoken hope is that if we can isolate "the truth and nothing but the truth," we'll develop a doctrinal critical mass that will mushroom and release spiritual energy. But such thinking gets to be a rut too. We have to keep cutting down and isolating, always finding a bit more error mixed in with the truth. Pretty soon we have nothing left to nurture us.

It's hard to generate momentum on our own. Despite our every effort, the biggest rut of all still remains—nothing is happening in our lives. Deep within our hearts we feel a need to experience intimacy with God, to see Him move in our lives. Nothing can replace that. We may try to live with the doldrums, may try to get by on a spiritual subsistence diet. But at some point we find ourselves silently screaming, "There's *got* to be more to it than this."

I wonder about those of us left in the sanctuary, staring up at that Easter banner. Surely sometimes, as we sing those hymns about power and triumph and transformation, some of us must wonder, "When are our lives going to match all the hype? Can the God of that banner really come down and shake things up? Is there anything at all supernatural about our day-to-day existence?"

I've thought about spiritual inertia a lot since losing Tad, since the best and the brightest among us shriveled up. Just how do we escape the doldrums? Can we really recapture that wonderful sense of intimacy, that first love? How does the "path of the righteous" become "like the first gleam of dawn, shining ever brighter till the full light of day" (Prov. 4:18)? How can a little mustard seed of faith truly become something grand, spreading its branches against the sky and providing a home for flocks of birds?

I've been trying to shape a clear answer for a long time, to have something to say to that empty pew that keeps staring back at me. Above all, I've needed answers in my own life.

Those answers didn't start to come until I took a journey back in time.

Chapter Two

Going Home Again

I drove through the dry hills of Riverside County toward my old college and the Christian Communicators' Conference I was to attend. Maybe it was the *Phantom of the Opera* tape I was listening to—those haunting Andrew Lloyd Webber songs about desire forever unfulfilled. Or maybe it was the old VW vans I saw on the road and the aging hippies still wandering after all these years. Whatever the reason, I arrived on campus primed for nostalgia, eager to visit the sites where I'd first been jolted into spiritual wakefulness.

Arriving early, I had time to kill before my first session. The dormitories and administration building looked about the same. I walked over to the chapel, where I'd first heard the student with the granny glasses and the surfer hair talk about "discovering" what I thought were the most ordinary things: how God accepts us, what salvation is all about. I'd heard the message a thousand times before. But he had made it all sound new, as if the Word had just dropped from some divine satellite and was going to change the world.

Next I passed the cafeteria, where I'd been hanging out when his friends invited me to a "different kind of prayer meeting." They had sounded extremely enthusiastic. At the time I couldn't imagine why. I could only picture a prayer meeting as three matrons and a grandfather kneeling for an hour and a half, then reading long passages from Deuteronomy. But I had gone anyway, unable to shake the feeling that something exciting had been set loose at school.

As I strolled down sidewalks near the women's dorm, I remembered a few exciting rendezvous and continued toward the edge of the campus. Somewhere, I knew, a long street led up a hill toward a small, white-framed house at the top. I recalled my fateful ascent to that house one evening under a moonless sky. The night sky had seemed vast, and I had felt vulnerable. I'd expected all kinds of things at the prayer meeting—except what greeted me when I walked in the door.

On the floor sat wall-to-wall students, all singing heartily. They welcomed me in with an easy courtesy. Sitting down, I listened to several lively tunes. It was clear that these kids meant every word, and they spoke my language. There wasn't a starched white shirt among them, none of the odd-ball fanaticism that I feared. Instead, an amiable spirit seemed to fill the room.

A student stood and began talking about how healthy relationships progress. He gave a beautiful picture of what God intended human oneness to be. Then the group prayed at the end—no trite speeches, just good conversation with the Lord. God seemed to be as close as the faces around me.

Afterward I started speaking with a stranger. We didn't go through the usual small talk that bounces between people at a party. It was as if right away we knew each other deeply. He told me about his recent "travels with the Lord." A whole personality, he was bright of eye, clear of mind, and mellowed by the Spirit.

Walking along the edge of the campus with these memories, I tried to recall what it had been like to first feel the spiritual barriers crumble. Before that night at the small white house, I'd been afraid of what the Spirit might do if He really got ahold of me. But afterward intimacy with God had seemed the most natural and exciting thing in the world.

Next I circled back to a smaller hill on campus, where a couple buddies and I had started praying together early each morning. It had been so astounding for me, overdosed on religion and turned off by everything that sounded like church, to find myself sharing real life with those guys and with God. The Lord had stepped out of the church manual and, for some inexplicable reason, had begun accompanying me to classes each day and hanging out in the dormitory at night.

Good memories. As I took my little private tour, I tried to taste what I had tasted years before. I wanted to experience it all over again, but it just wasn't there. I couldn't get it back.

The chapel was locked. The cafeteria had been drastically redecorated and stood empty. I had no clue as to where the white house on the hill might be. The hillside where we'd prayed had been landscaped beyond recognition. And the dormitory where I'd stayed that freshman year was now collapsing.

As I checked into a guest room, I felt struck by the distance between what had once happened to me in that place before and where I stood in the present. It wasn't just the exterior landscape that had changed—it was the landscape in the heart. I wasn't the same person. During the communication conference I had a lot to say about script writing, about the best ways of presenting the gospel, and about how to relate contemporary issues to biblical truths. But I couldn't help wondering if I was, in a way, speaking from the sidelines. A mature Christian, I had the theory down, the technique . . . But what about the fire? What about the heady sense of encountering God that I had once known? Was I really in the game anymore?

Most of us find out, at some point or another, that we can't really go home again. The greatest spiritual hits of our youth are not reproducible. We've changed. "Home" has altered even more.

And yet we still can't shake the longing to go back. "Spiritual maturity" must have more to it than this.

Many of us who go through middle age begin to feel an intense longing for intimacy. Sometimes it remains in the background, a dull pain. Other times it takes the form of frantic love affairs. Occasionally we switch jobs or addresses. But always there remains that haunting feeling—life has got to have more to it than this. It becomes especially keen when we realize we can't go home again. After my short stay in Calkins Hall I decided that you just can't rekindle the same old fire. That belongs to another time and another place.

But then I went back to high school.

GOING HOME AGAIN

As soon as I walked into Suite 1609 at the hotel, it was one gasp of recognition after another. Suddenly faces from my 20-year-old yearbook burst into life again. Ann was a little pudgier, but with the same guileless charm; Don, still quietly amiable; Donna, still bright and confident. Becky's little-girl voice belied the fact that she teaches at a Michigan medical school. Brad's familiar gawky mannerisms did not suggest that he is a corporate vice president.

A few times during this rush of a twentieth-year reunion, a face would come up to greet me and I would draw a blank. It was like being accosted by a stranger on the street. But then they'd start talking and gesturing, and the personality I had known at the age of 17 would suddenly materialize in front of me, tangible and intact.

We milled about, catching up on two decades, with all the fervor of bull market traders on the floor of the stock exchange. Most of us didn't crash until 3:00 in the morning.

The next day the group set off to visit our boarding academy campus. The administration building and dorms looked the same, but they'd built a new chapel. We peered into the old assembly room, where we'd watched terrible instructional movies and paraded down the hall where the principal had frowned at our faded jeans, asking whether we would wear overalls to school if allowed. Then we sat down in the history class in which the teacher once put his hand over the film projector as "Thomas Jefferson" kissed his wife goodbye.

Wandering over the campus, we found ourselves tracking through the backwoods of religion, revisiting old legalistic haunts, the site of a painfully constricted faith. We recalled that most of our peers who'd sat in the old chapel couldn't wait to get out from under God's thumb.

But then we had our own version of chapel. We decided to share what had been going on in our lives. I talked about how fellow student Bill Shelley had changed my life, about how winsome he'd made religious goodness appear. Barbara spoke about finding a great church where she was enjoying worship for the first time in her life. Becky told us about how she was clinging to God through her husband's midlife crisis. More and more people shared, and suddenly I realized with a start that this was better than before! Most of us could not have imagined, back then in that uptight religious corner of the world, what real spirituality could be like. But many of my classmates had found a way to get connected.

By the time our reunion worship service began, my head was full of stories. A lot of skeletons had been fleshed out. Our old Bible teacher gave the sermon. His voice occasionally short-circuited, but the man could still issue a strong appeal. He told us he wanted to see the class of 1970 all together in heaven—wanted another reunion up there, without anyone left out of the circle. The girls started passing out tissues. The guys nodded soberly. At the end we stood with our arms around each other and promised that, yes, we would be there. Then we were singing with lively voices, standing almost wall to wall. Chapel had never sounded like this before.

SOME THINGS NEVER CHANGE

My 20-year reunion gave me quite a dose of hope. It started me thinking that maybe you *can* go home again. Maybe it can be even better than before. Our class sustained plenty of casualties, to be sure. Quite a few had burned out on being good. But those who remained had done more than survive. Sparks loitering in those middle-aged hearts just waited to be fanned into flame. For a few moments we were part of an intimate circle.

That reunion showed me something vital about my own quest. It hit me while I was flying back to California. I'd been in a rush all weekend, processing one story after another. But once I had time to slow down, wonder overcame me. So much had happened since my classmates and I had been together. The hippies were still out in force when we paraded in our green graduation gowns. The Vietnam War still raged; Watergate had yet to spread its scandal.

In the two decades since we'd parted, Ford, Carter, and Reagan had served their terms. The oil embargo had come and gone. The nation had experienced a recession and layoffs, followed by the junk bond and leveraged buyout frenzy.

But through all this history, through all the earthshaking events that defined our times, those faces from high school persisted. I couldn't get over it. The personalities seemed like artifacts from a lost civilization. The texture of a voice, the gesture of a hand, the expression of a countenance—I turned them over and over in my mind's eye, amazed at how perfectly they'd been preserved. Nothing else mattered. It was as if nothing else of significance had happened during the 20-year interval.

At that moment I felt the enormous weight of God's personhood. The Creator, the fountain of all personalities, persists through all history, through everything that happens. He's the same God who used the student with the granny glasses and surfer hair to jolt me awake. The same God who met me in that little white house on the hill. The eternal nature of God is, of course, a truism. I have always known this. But that day on the plane I could feel it.

Frequently we talk about trying to get close to God, about attempting to bridge the gap, about God seeming to be remote. But after my reunion, I realized that God hasn't gone anywhere. He's exactly where He always was, as close to us as ever.

It's our capacity to absorb the divine presence that has suffered. Our ability to grasp what is in front of our faces has slipped. God is as big and bold and exciting as He always was. Only our hearts have narrowed and grown a bit stuffier.

EMBRACING THE INTIMATE GOD

I need a deeper heart—that's the basic requirement for recapturing a sense of intimacy with God. I need more room in there for the "fountain of personality" to flow and flood my being. On that plane heading home I felt almost as if my insides were bursting, so much had been crammed in there. I had made room for so many faces, sensing how infinitely valuable each person was, and it caused an almost violent deepening of my heart.

Something similar needs to happen in my relationship with God. I need to experience that same kind of yanking and stretching in my spiritual life, making more room for intimacy with Him.

The New Testament passage that perhaps most graphically pictures a sense of intimacy with God is Ephesians 3:18, 19. In it Paul prays that believers may "grasp how wide and long and high and deep is the love of Christ," and then "know this love that surpasses knowledge" that they "may be filled to the measure of all the fullness of God."

In genuine intimacy we know and experience the full dimensions of one another's love. It's an understanding that surpasses mere knowledge, filling us up in a way that somehow mirrors the "fullness of God."

Verses 16 and 17 of this passage from Ephesians suggest how we can grow into this kind of intimacy: "I pray that out of his glorious riches [the Father] may strengthen you with power through his Spirit in your inner being, so that Christ may dwell in your hearts through faith."

We believers need that strengthening with power in our inner beings. Something must happen to the state of our hearts. That's the prerequisite to being "filled to the measure of all the fullness of God."

The fact is that we just can't accept all that God wants to give us. In our present condition we simply can't grasp the height and depth and breadth of His love or absorb much of His presence. But it's not a problem of God being too remote or a matter of His unwillingness to pour Himself out in full measure. Rather it stems from the incapacity of our hearts to receive. We need to be strengthened—to be deepened.

In the same Epistle Paul prays that "the eyes of your heart may be enlightened in order that you may know the hope to which he has called you" (Eph. 1:18). Again, it's the state of our hearts that makes the difference. We need more than an intellectual grasp of God's truth if we are to experience intimacy. Seeing ever more clearly with the eyes of our hearts, we will be stretched and strengthened and deepened so we can embrace the intimate God.

God deepens our hearts in various ways—through emotional struggles, relationships, misfortunes, and our devotional lives. His basic tool is life itself. The more we cooperate with His work, the more fully we can experience intimacy. It's the quality of our relationships and devotional life, and the way in which we respond to misfortunes and emotional challenges, that make the difference.

But don't think that intimacy with God requires some unusual, heroic effort. Don't assume it happens only to the mystically inclined. You don't have to go to some exotic sacred spot to recapture that sense of closeness with God. It's right there beside you, and can start right now. God is eager to deepen your heart so He can pour in His fullness.

That's what this book is about. It's a personal odyssey, a description of what has been most helpful in my own struggles and the struggles of others who have embarked on that most wonderful of journeys toward "the surpassing greatness of knowing Christ."

Part Two

*Obstacles to
Deepening Our Hearts*

Chapter Three

Clear Away the Clutter

One long Sunday afternoon years ago I was traveling with my Aunt Margaret across the flat midsection of Texas toward a Christmas reunion with relatives in Houston. As we drove, I began telling her about all the thrilling religious things happening at college. I was excited because all the Christian clichés people had been throwing at me all my life were finally turning into flesh-and-blood reality. Religious platitudes had turned into discipleship. We weren't just nodding assent to that vaguely disturbing duty to "witness," but were doing it—and having wonderful encounters with other students. God seemed very much alive and well on the campus of Western Illinois University.

Aunt Margaret listened appreciatively and asked questions about how it all worked. In particular she wanted the nitty-gritty details about my "daily walk with Christ." Her questions surprised me a bit. The woman had gone to church all her life and seemed well acquainted with the facts of the faith. I remembered sitting on her lap as a kid and listening to her read from *The Bible Story,* by Arthur Maxwell. My aunt always seemed to be holding Jesus' hand.

But now it appeared as if she had to figure it out all over again. I spoke of how inspiring the Bible had become for me since I was actually using it. She kept asking how the devotional life could work. But the more I explained, the more difficult the concept seemed for her to grasp.

Sometimes Margaret would take a deep breath and point out something important about the scenery. "Here's where Sam Houston made a move against the Mexican army. There's a grove of hickory, part of a vast legacy from one of Texas' early governors."

But as the Texas grasslands flew by, we kept slipping back to her big question: How does it all work? She spoke admiringly of people who were close to God, yet real faith appeared out of reach for her. I waxed euphoric about justification by faith, an ancient truth that in one deft stroke had severed all the knots that legalism had once tied in my head. The security of placing my faith firmly in Christ seemed to settle everything for me. But she couldn't quite get it. How do you know that your faith is genuine? How can you be sure that you have a "saving relationship"?

It was frustrating. We talked for hours, but I couldn't quite get through to Aunt Margaret.

On subsequent visits to Texas I had similar experiences. Aunt Margaret and I would go to church together. I'd stop by her house to visit and talk about what was happening in my life. She'd listen appreciatively, always making me feel at home in her tidy living room full of art books and mementos from her travels overseas. The woman always had charming anecdotes to tell. But when it came to "that relationship thing," growing close to God, it always seemed that she was a tourist admiring a slightly exotic culture. Somehow she could never quite go native.

One year I learned with dismay that Aunt Margaret's marriage had fallen apart. She and Uncle Zack managed an amicable divorce. They wanted to spare the relatives the unpleasant details. But in the months that followed, those details began to slip out anyway. Deep hurts rose to the surface and asked for a little tea and sympathy.

Most shocking of all was the skeleton that stood up and walked right out of the closet. Margaret had been involved in sexual immorality—something I tried hard not to believe, not about the woman who'd read from the *Bible Story* books, with all those pictures of Jesus.

But the details kept coming, and the stories got worse. It evidently was a problem that went back a long way, and Aunt Margaret had kept it hidden. She'd never been able to deal with it head-on.

I don't know if this particular issue led to the divorce—or even if it was a major cause. But I do think it helped me understand a little about why Aunt Margaret kept asking questions without getting answers, why she could never quite get close to God.

It wasn't that God took a particular dislike to this sin and so kept her at a distance. He was eager to forgive Aunt Margaret just as He was eager to forgive me for all my mistakes. But she apparently just couldn't lay her problem out on the table. Keeping it in a dark corner produced in her a chronic sense of disconnection from God.

GUILT: THE HIDDEN ENEMY

When it comes to the closeness we need, there is no more lethal adversary than unresolved guilt. Guilt kills intimacy. It will always sabotage our efforts to work on the relationship thing. We may come to God again and again, in all sorts of ways, but if we're hiding something from Him in our hearts, our hearts can never deepen. He can't begin to strengthen us in our innermost beings until He has access to our innermost beings.

Usually, when we start out in the Christian life, we bare our souls to God. Everything's out in the open. We chuck our miserable pasts and open ourselves up to His promising future. But as the years go by, human nature tends to acquire blind spots, pet habits, secret sins. Our defenses become more sophisticated. We go from fighting the good fight to waging a cold war to just coping with sin. And once a problem gets buried, guilt percolates to the surface in all kinds of unhealthy ways.

The prospect of intimacy with God, which we desire so much, can threaten us with exposure at the same time. And so we may find ourselves clinging to Him with one hand and pushing Him away with the other.

Although we long for intimacy, we also fear exposure. I've sensed this tension in people extremely close to me. They hear a powerful sermon on God's love, something that sweeps a whole congregation into the arms of the Father. But they remain only politely appreciative: "That was a nice talk." They seem unable to grasp the wonderful grace plopped down on their laps. I talk to them, try to pour more on—seeking to show how lavishly God expends His mercy and love on us. I tell them just to accept it.

But as they hold out their hands, their wrists go limp. They can't bring themselves to absorb God's gracious love—simply can't afford to get that close to Him. That hidden thing warns them off. So they feel compelled to keep the Lord at arm's length. While they can talk about God, the loving Father, from a distance, when He passes close by, they feel His face taking on the expression of a highway patrolman. That dark blot on their record makes His most earnest appeals sound like accusations.

GETTING IT ALL OUT

A key step toward achieving real intimacy is laying our problems out on the table. We've got to be transparent; we've got to open up our hearts in order for God to deepen them. That's why God gives us this wonderful thing called confession.

It hit me one day during my freshman year in college. I'd been learning in psychology class about all the mental "unhealth" that human beings are prone to. Suddenly I realized that confession can clear away an incredible amount of dysfunction. I don't have to hide anything or blame anyone. Nor do I have to compensate, sublimate, atone for, disguise, counterattack, deny, project, vent, or repress. I don't have to do anything except confess. Calling myself a sinner before a holy God now struck me as a wonderfully liberating thing. Sweeping away a mountain of clutter, it gave me a simple, clean starting point.

Sometimes we build up layers of defense around our weaknesses or go through complicated efforts to hide our faults. But the solution can be quite simple: confession—honesty before God, with nothing held back.

It's interesting to note that the Greek word for "confess" used in the New Testament literally means to assent or to agree. Confessing our sins means that we agree with God about them. We say, "Yes, You're right in pointing out this action as wrong."

Biblical confession is not the equivalent of wallowing in our sins. Nor is it an act of penance done to earn forgiveness. Certainly we express our sorrow for what we've done. But most of all, we give assent—we agree with God. We accept both our guilt and His forgiving mercy.

Only when we refuse to look at specific wrongs does guilt spread inside us and take on a depressing vagueness. And it's only when we close our eyes and turn away that it starts shrinking our hearts. Guilt denied only multiplies. Countless anxious thoughts incapacitate us. We miss opportunities for intimacy again and again.

BACKING UP TO THE WINDOW

Because many of us expend so much energy putting on a good front for other people, we sometimes unwittingly try the same strategy with God. After all, we smile pleasantly in church and act like the perfect Christian (nobody wants to air their dirty laundry before other believers). So we start thinking that we should create the right impression for the Lord, too. What we don't realize is that nothing exposes us before God so much as the act of covering up.

One day as I was walking from the parking lot toward a hospital to pay someone a visit I caught a startling glimpse through one of the second-floor windows. A patient had just stood up to greet a couple who'd walked through the door of his room. He had one of those infamous hospital gowns draped around his shoulders and began fumbling with it—since he had nothing else on. The man was modestly backing away from his friends as he tried to spread the gown down in front of him.

What he didn't realize was that he'd backed right up to a large floor-length window. As he stood there talking to his friends, thinking himself entirely covered, he had exposed his lily-white posterior to the many citizens of our community entering the hospital at that moment.

The Bible repeatedly informs us that God has a large window into our innermost hearts. We may think we've got ourselves pretty well covered, as we adjust external appearances for the benefit of a few friends. But we're really backing up to a window and revealing ourselves to a much more significant audience. Heaven sees it all.

So what's the point of concealing it? Why the pretense? Amos reminds us that God could find us even if we were to flee to the bottom of the sea (Amos 9:3). Jeremiah asks what the point is of hiding in some "secret place" if the Lord fills the heaven and the earth (Jer. 23:24)?

God identified Himself to Solomon as the one who "searches every heart and understands every motive behind the thoughts" (1 Chron. 28:9). Solomon needed to hear this, because later he used his great intelligence to rationalize all kinds of pagan worship among his wives. He may have thought it all took place in the privacy of his harem, but he was just backing up to the window.

Sometimes we tell ourselves that we must keep things hidden in order to avoid scandal. We're afraid that real honesty will lead to humiliation. But the pain we may have to face now is nothing compared to the scandal some will surely face at the judgment. Referring to that day, Paul wrote, "He will bring to light what is hidden in darkness and will expose the motives of men's hearts" (1 Cor. 4:5).

When Jesus spoke against hypocrisy, He said, "There is nothing concealed that will not be disclosed, or hidden that will not be made known. What you have said in the dark will be heard in the daylight, and what you have whispered in the ear in the inner rooms will be proclaimed from the roofs" (Luke 12:2, 3).

It's far better to confess now than be exposed later, to walk straight into the prayer closet than to back up to the window. God needs our permission to move inside us and expand our hearts. Confession gives Him that access, an important step toward intimacy. That's why God links His great calls to confession and repentance to His covenant love. Remember His appeal through the prophet Jeremiah: " 'Only acknowledge your guilt. . . . Return, faithless people,' declares the Lord, 'for I am your husband. I will choose you . . . and bring you to Zion' " (Jer. 3:13, 14).

Why should we acknowledge our guilt? Not because God needs to put us in our place or make a point of His moral superiority, but because He wants that kind of intimate relationship.

The apostle John expresses this in terms of God's faithfulness: "If we confess our sins, he is faithful and just and will forgive us our sins and purify us from all unrighteousness" (1 John 1:9). We confess because our God is faithful and we can trust Him with our innermost secrets. He will never take advantage of our vulnerability, but will always respond with forgiveness and cleansing.

ONE DEEPENED HEART

Sonia started out life as a happy, expansive child. But at the age of 12 she lost her beloved mother, and her gloomy, uncommunicative dad wasn't there to help her emotionally through the shock. The girl withdrew into her own lonely world. Then, just when she thought she might be able to take her mother's place around the house, her dad remarried. Rebelling against her stepmother, Sonia criticized everything about her.

At the age of 14 Sonia came down with pneumonia. The next year she suffered through an attack of influenza.

A few years later Sonia decided to become a teacher in order to leave home. She did finish her education and training, but through her 20s she suffered from all kinds of ailments: pleurisy, bronchitis, ulcers, tuberculosis. Her emotional life also remained in a turmoil. Although always anxious about her family, she remained isolated from it.

Sonia became a miserable and friendless young woman. But one day someone sent her to see yet another doctor. This time it was Christian physician Paul Tournier. After going over her case history, he realized that what Sonia needed was a strong spirit to sustain her body.

During subsequent sessions with Dr. Tournier, Sonia shared more and more of her personal story. Finally, after praying together, they came to the root of her problems: she needed to confess something. Looking into her anguished face, the physician could tell she was going through a great spiritual battle. Sonia had tried twice before to get this thing out before Christian friends, but had been unable to speak.

Now she finally unburdened herself. It was a wrong she'd committed in childhood, something secret, something forgotten by everyone who thought her life irreproachable. But it had haunted her all her life. And deep in her mind she knew that behind the pleurisy and influenza, behind the ulcers and the pneumonia, lay this dark thing.

There in the doctor's study Sonia let it go before God. She made her confession. And Dr. Tournier helped her make a consecration of her life to Jesus Christ, acknowledging His forgiveness.

Sonia still had her struggles. She had been carrying emotional baggage around for a long time. But now she started making progress. Ceasing to blame her stepmother for ruining her life, she took responsibility for her resentment. Her emotional life evened out, her physical health steadily improved, and she began to grow spiritually. As Dr. Tournier put it: "The current of her spiritual life, freed from the great obstacle that had obstructed it until that time, began to carry along with it lesser debris."

That current proved strong indeed. It moved her past the loss of a teaching position, enabling her to accept the disappointment "quite simply and calmly." And it transformed her most difficult relationships. Dr. Tournier observed that Sonia became "a pillar of strength to her family" and began to "exercise a spiritual influence on those around her."

God can use simple confession as a powerful tool in our lives. It clears away an enormous amount of emotional clutter. And the blank slate that follows is the space in which intimacy with God can grow. Only the transparent hearts can begin to deepen.

Chapter Four

Respond With a Self

I used to drive a forklift in a furniture factory warehouse, retrieving flats of deacon benches, hope chests, and six-drawer dressers, and delivering them to Arthur, a man of indeterminate age, who then loaded the boxed pine furniture into neat stacks in a railroad boxcar. Arthur seemed physically incapable of hurrying, his movements as deliberate as a minute hand on a watch. But he wasn't at all lazy. In fact, you almost never found him at rest. Boxcar after boxcar, trailer after trailer—he filled them with a peculiar intensity.

Arthur was so different from me—17 and erratically active, racing around on my forklift, clambering over 40-foot-high stacks in the warehouse for a stray deacon bench, dodging the staples of the piecework guys gunning for me. I often dropped things. Entire stacks of dressers tumbled down on the roof of my forklift, much to the boss's dismay. Arthur never dropped things. He just kept plodding along, arms thick and solid from labor, skin darkened by the sun, expecting nothing more than sweat in this life.

Once in a while I tried talking with him, but could never really get beyond his benign and slightly nervous exterior. He seemed always to be avoiding himself, gently turning aside personal questions as if someone had made an indecent remark. During breaktime he remained in the corner, out of the way, never really in a conversation, always commenting from the edge. I had the impression that Arthur was a religious man, reverent from a long distance. Among his profane coworkers Arthur would go out of his way to avoid the appearance of evil, but he never preached at anyone.

Arthur seemed the embodiment of humility to me, always self-effacing. At the same time it distressed me that I could never put a finger on the self that hid somewhere within his striped overalls. In my idealistic youth I felt a keen desire for Arthur to be somebody, but he remained deliberately overshadowed, consciously hiding his identity, never letting it surface. I glimpsed in his weathered features a measure of self-hatred.

I still don't know what made him tick. But he sticks in my mind as a haunting image of a dark kind of humility.

FINDING THE "I" IN "I LOVE YOU"

One of the prerequisites for intimacy with God is having a definite self that can relate to Him. We need a personality with which to respond to this ultimate personality. It's an obvious point, but one that many Christians have missed throughout history.

Quite a few mystics, in fact, have tried to obliterate the self, to remove everything personal in their lives, hoping that in the resulting emptiness they might find God. For some reason I've always had an aversion to this method of finding Him by subtracting from ourselves. It suggests that God is so elusive a presence that we can detect Him only through complete sensory deprivation.

The Lord does advise us to "be still, and know that I am God" (Ps. 46:10). Meditative silence does have its place. But He didn't command us to "be nil and know that I am God."

We need to have a sense of self in order to capture a sense of intimacy. God wants to deepen our hearts in order to fill us with the length and breadth and depth of His love. So it won't do much good to write off our hearts as worthless.

Arthur is an extreme example of one obstacle to intimacy. But another obstacle lurks on the opposite side of the spectrum. While we shouldn't exile the innermost self as the enemy, neither should we cling to it as a savior. People completely absorbed in themselves don't have much luck with intimacy, either. When everything gets sucked up into the self, the result is a kind of implosion.

BUT ENOUGH ABOUT YOU . . . LET'S TALK ABOUT ME

Jake was such a case. I met him one day as he was hustling at church for bus fare. His greasy hair hung limp, his face was an unearthly off-white, and his shirt and pants appeared to be having some kind of argument. Even from a distance he could not hide that tentative shuffle of the emotionally disturbed.

The man quickly won my sympathy. His eyes never rested on any one object, and he could speak only in barely audible bursts, sentences rushing out as if on a brief prison furlough. His self-conscious hands fumbled constantly for a natural gesture that never came.

He had a lot to be self-conscious about. And he queried me obsessively about what people were thinking of him—that boy over there, that woman glancing his way. It seemed like a perfectly rational concern at the time. After all, he was a spectacle, displaying the abused look of those always ready to dodge a blow to the psyche.

I tried to help, jumping confidently into chaos. He always needed to go somewhere, so I took him around for a while and came up with dimes for phone calls and with bus fare now and then so he could wander off from home to meet reluctant friends. This adolescent in his mid-30s persisted in asking, knocking, seeking (like a good Christian), and I responded on occasion. But his desires were always pitifully focused on the immediate moment—getting away, getting the ride, getting his way, thus avoiding other considerations at all costs. I couldn't get any meaning out of him.

So I turned behaviorist and tried to force one healthy conversation into his jittery thoughts. We went over simple questions that people ask each other: How have you been? Did you have a good day? Jake was not mentally disabled, but his feverish concentration on the thing he wanted right now consumed all normal interaction. If only I could get him just once to show a flicker of interest in another person. But each time we managed a few spurts of dialogue, the conversation quickly collapsed into the bottomless abyss of his self.

Jake turned out to be a heartbreaking, maddening tragedy. He manipulated total strangers for all they were worth. Although forever running away from the horror of himself, he always got caught more deeply in it.

Of course, we recommended counseling. But he was deathly afraid of it, terrified that those smooth talkers only wanted a reason to lock him up. We begged and assured and bribed and set up meetings and threatened—to no avail. He promised and lied (the two seemed indistinguishable) his way from one momentary impulse to the next.

The man demonstrated self-awareness with a vengeance, his thoughts always spinning in that vortex. No impulse could drift out of it to take root in human or divine nourishment. He was the most self-centered person I have ever known, and the most profoundly disturbed. I don't think that was coincidental.

In Henrik Ibsen's *Peer Gynt* the mad director of an asylum declares:

> "We're ourselves and nothing but ourselves
> We speed full sail ahead as ourselves,
> We shut ourselves up in a keg of self.
> We stew in our own juice . . .
> And get seasoned in a well of self. . . .
> There are no thoughts or sorrows outside our own."

We can fall off the cliff either way: by destroying a sense of self or by getting lost in it. Neither extreme will help to deepen our souls. Whether we're considering our hearts as demons or worshiping "the god within," we fail to make room for the real thing that will fill us up.

Both extremes point to one basic problem: insecurity, the lack of a healthy sense of self. They are frantic attempts to fill up the holes in our hearts. Usually they result from a lack of love and nurture in childhood. People who haven't received enough affirmation are always trying to get what they need from others. Yet one of the tragedies of life is that the less love a person receives during formative years, the harder it is later to take in the love he or she so desperately needs.

Lack of love doesn't just leave our hearts empty—it causes them to shrink over time. We lose our capacity to receive the very thing we so desperately need. Although we try to absorb all the wonderful talk about the love of a heavenly Father, it doesn't quite sink in.

So how do we get started? How do we escape the two tragedies of Arthur and Jake?

TRAVELING OUT OF THE SELF

In an old scratched photograph one can see Charles de Foucauld at the age of 6 dressed in hunting costume and holding a toy gun, sulky and truculent, staring out at the world. That faded image proved to be a prophetic portrayal. Through the rest of his childhood Charles established a record as a violent-tempered and domineering boy. Later as a fat slothful adolescent, his family sent him to a Jesuit boarding school in Paris, where he became (from a later perspective) "wholly an egotist, wholly vain, totally impious," and, because he came from a good family, was politely expelled.

At 21 Charles, having made a clean break with religion, became a sublieutenant with the Hussars. His military duties were light, he had lots of money, and he was able to entertain friends in a richly furnished apartment, showing off a succession of expensive mistresses at lavish parties.

Years later Charles would recall, "I felt a painful void, an anguish and a sorrow . . . each evening as soon as I found myself alone in my apartment; it was this that held me dumb, depressed, during what people call entertainments." The sublieutenant could never fill that void within.

But Charles began to notice something special about a cousin named Marie. She always seemed to make the Christian life appear a delight and an adventure. He couldn't escape the contrast between her life and his. One day he told her wistfully, "How lucky you are in your faith."

But that luck was making its way surely toward him. Charles began dropping into churches to check up on the faith he'd abandoned. Something inside him prompted him to request, "My God, if You exist, make me know You."

One evening a popular priest named Abbe Huvelin came to the De Foucauld home. Distinguished guests often attended the family's social affairs. Whenever Huvelin preached the church was packed. His combination of sanctity and intelligence had a magnetic influence on his contemporaries. Introduced to Huvelin, Charles liked him immediately. He listened intently as the man began to share what Christ's religion was all about.

Soon after that visit, Charles confessed his sins and received Communion. With the help of Huvelin he clambered over the remaining intellectual obstacles to faith and then fell under the spell of a divine perspective: "As soon as I believed there was a God, I knew I could not do otherwise than to live only for Him. God is so great! There is such a difference between God and all that is not He."

Finally Charles had found something big enough to consume his vanity and overpower his voracious ego. His indulgent self found an exit from its own pettiness and anguish. Eventually Charles expressed this radical and quickening escape by serving as a Trappist monk in the Sahara and adopting a minimalist lifestyle.

In the middle of the desert, near a lonely French army post, he built a rustic chapel of palm beams. "Very poor," Charles admitted, "but harmonious and pretty." Four palm trunks held up the roof, and a paraffin lamp threw light on the altar. He drew the 14 stations of the cross on packing case boards, and on white calico painted a large figure of Christ "stretching out His arms to embrace, to clasp, to call all men, and give Himself for all."

Visiting desert settlements, Charles encountered proud, veiled Tuareg warriors as well as hungry nomads afflicted with ulcerated eyes, malaria, typhus, and gangrenous cuts. Slowly the Trappist earned their trust. They came to delight in the wiry holy man who spoke their language, required neither flattery nor gifts, but happily bestowed medicines, soap, flour, sugar, tea, and needles on them. One woman whose child Charles had saved from death declared, "How terrible it is to think of a man so good, so charitable, going to hell because he is not a Muslim!"

Among those who came to the chapel to chat were Black slaves who exhibited raw ankles, chained wrists, cheeks branded like a camel's, and backs scarred from lashes. Charles could not be silent. The penniless priest began begging and cajoling his superiors for money so he could purchase slaves and set them free.

It's quite remarkable to see how far from the once fat, indulgent, vain little self the man had traveled. The man who had grown up amid aristocratic ease endured the harsh desert and his own even harsher discipline with an easy cheerfulness, because when in prayer he saw that his Lord was infinitely happy and lacked nothing—"Then I, too, am happy, and I lack nothing; Your happiness suffices me."

His intimacy with his Lord gave Charles a profound security in his calling. He never insisted that others copy his ascetic lifestyle. When he sent a young Tuareg to France for a visit, he carefully arranged that everything would be pleasant and comfortable for him there. While traveling with a certain Brother Michael, Charles would cover him with his own cloak during the night, explaining to others that he was hardened to the desert cold, and he sent the brother off for coffee and barley cake in the morning although he himself never had breakfast.

Charles submitted himself to a highly demanding religious rule, but the way he centered all on God made it seem effortless. "He holds up equally my soul and my body," he assured friends. "I have nothing to carry; He carries it all."

On those rare occasions when Charles found someone who could understand something of his feelings, he tried to share "the immense happiness which one enjoys at the thought that God is God and that He whom we love with our whole being is infinitely and eternally blessed."

After Charles's death at the hands of rogue tribesmen, one could sum up his life in the few possessions discovered at his chapel: a breviary, a cross, a chalice, linen, and candlesticks. That was all. They formed an eloquent still life, each object essential in the composition, laid out with passionate conviction.

FINDING A NEW FOCUS

People experience a profound security when they invest their energy in admiring God. Healthy self-esteem is not something we do to ourselves or can really give ourselves. It grows out of admiring someone greater than ourselves, something we absorb in a relationship with God.

Insecure people are always wrapped up in themselves. Whether excessively humble or excessively proud, self remains at the center. And it's terribly difficult to break away from that desperate defensive preoccupation. Charles de Foucauld acquired a healthy sense of self because he had been captivated by a great God. Escaping himself, he stood constantly in awe that a person could embrace God. He simply admired the divine too much ever to be caught posing self-consciously as the humble holy man.

The kind of security we experience has a lot to do with the kind of humility we have. We need to absorb the fact that God is a sovereign, separate being. He is a significant other who gives us an identity. It won't do to conjure up some divine essence, inherent in our souls, as God. Saying that we're all God and that God is in all of us may sound encouraging at first, but the concept falls apart in the end. If God is all things, in everything equally, then we've just labeled the world differently—we've just put a higher sticker price on the same old car. Proclaiming that God is everything is ultimately not much different from saying that God is nothing.

The biblical distinction between Creator and creature is important here. God is intimately related to us, but He is *not* us. He is a separate individual seeking genuine relationships with other separate individuals. Healthy self-esteem does not result from the self claiming squatters' rights on divinity, but from the self relating to someone greater.

Another essential quality of the God of Scripture is His holiness. God's passion for justice blends with His compassion for imperfect individuals. The accepting God who gives people self-worth is not a moral pushover. The Bible presents Him as a consuming fire of righteousness, upright in all His ways, faithful to generation after generation.

Again, what matters is *who* accepts us, not just that we are accepted.

ONE WHO MADE IT ALL WORTHWHILE

During his senior year of high school a student named Ben slipped into the habit of contemplating the meaning of life and, as a result, grew somewhat suicidal. The usual idealism of youth ground against the usual disasters in the world. To Ben it hardly seemed worthwhile to pursue an education or a career—or even a life. Every choice seemed compromise. School had exposed him to the prevailing psychological theme of value-free acceptance. But he couldn't bring himself to accept it. It was a lie to give in to evil, a lie to say that things were OK. That's why he began toying with the idea of ending it all.

But then amid his gloomy philosophical rumblings came the thought: *If there was just one man who had lived a completely good life, it would be worth it all.* Ben had seen plenty of evidence that even the best of humanity hid pockets of cruelty. But what if there were an exception? That would make a difference.

For a while Ben carried that thought around as his last argument against suicide. Then he spent a holiday at his aunt's house. The Christian woman, without saying anything, reminded him of his childhood days in church. All those stories about Jesus came back to him. Themes long dormant awakened, and suddenly he realized that this was precisely his answer: Jesus was the completely good man who made life worthwhile.

Ben didn't kill himself. Years later I met him in college and enjoyed the pleasure of his company as a fellow believer. He'd found a relationship with this Good Man.

It is a holy God who extends to us His gracious regard. That makes an enormous difference. He gives human beings a sense of freedom and dignity by the way He relates to them. It won't do just to have some benign blob in the sky who hands out greeting cards to the indifferent masses. Unfortunately, a lot of people have reduced God to the fast-food essentials: He loves everybody, so slide in and out whenever convenient on greasy, value-free acceptance. "I'll take mine without that high-fiber part about holiness, please."

Indulgence doesn't produce security—it simply gives the self-centered an ever-constricting circle to play in. Big egos thrive in part by forming private alliances with some malleable deity up in the sky. They project their whims up as the divine will.

Those who live securely, however, sense their responsibility before a God of law. They don't just look up at a frozen smile, but bow before a righteous Lord. Such men and women sincerely admire the holy God who has chosen them.

Healthy security has to have this combination: righteous expectations and loving acceptance. The God of the Bible expresses both consistently and intensely. He has created each one of us for the good life. God doesn't institutionalize us, abandon us to some ghetto for the morally deficient, tell us that it's OK we can't make it, that we're only human. No, God believes in us and has high hopes for us and wants us to fulfill those hopes.

But He also catches us when we fall, accepting our frailty and forgiving our moral stumblings. He is able to love us when we're at our worst—and still hope. God's ardent expressions of justice and mercy produce a profound sense of security in those who bow before Him. They experience healthy humility. And this humility, in turn, opens them up to more mercy and justice.

We bow before a God who loves us. The ultimate Significant Other, who can give us a secure identity, He is the infinitely great individual whose love for us is infinitely intense. That's security.

The value we give ourselves is directly proportionate to the value placed on us by the people we most regard. The acceptance of drinking buddies is nice, but generally produces no great sense of self-worth. The love of a father, on the other hand, is of tremendous importance. So when a holy God cherishes us and we can hold on to that cherishing steadily, as Charles did, the result is a wealth of security. We find a self-worth rich enough to give away, and an identity that can blossom in the desert.

There is a way to fill up the holes in our hearts. We can break out of that tragic predicament of failing again and again to absorb love because we don't receive it in our formative years. It's not a matter of trying to do something to ourselves as much as it is a matter of doing something toward God: investing our emotional energy in admiring Him. Each of us needs to rediscover His winsome qualities for ourselves. If we keep our eyes open, He will reveal Himself to us in the most unexpected places.

HOMESICK FOR THE UNLOVABLE

Our summer camp was a luscious green. Set around a shimmering, cool lake, it harbored all kinds of delights for kids: canoe rides, waterskiing, horseback riding, crafts, and campfires. A fresh new world of cattails, hickory, and bullfrogs invited exploration. In between scheduled activities some pillow fight or game of kick-the-can kept things hopping.

But my cabin had one 9-year-old who wasn't completely happy in this paradise. Something kept gnawing at Billy, especially as he lay on his bunk after lights out. Finally the red-haired, freckled-faced boy unburdened himself to me. "I think I've learned enough now. I think they need me at home."

"Billy, don't you think your folks can manage without you for a week?" I asked.

"And the food here is kind of funny," he continued.

"You don't like the food?"

"Well . . . I may get sick."

"You look pretty healthy to me."

"But I don't feel so good."

"That's too bad—out here in all this fresh air, with the trees and squirrels and—"

"And yesterday I cut my finger—see?"

"Just a scratch, Billy."

"You know, it could be real dangerous out here . . ." The boy paused and looked out the window. "I think my mother needs me."

After failing to convince Billy of the wonderful time he was having at camp, I informed the camp director. Mr. Logan, however, wanted his camper to stick it out for the duration. He believed homesickness was an emotional barrier that needed to be hurdled, lest it get harder the next time around. So the man invited Billy into his office for a little chat.

The boy was quiet and polite, but not even the camp director's try-it-just-one-more-day offer could release the boy's white-knuckled grasp on the hope of going home *now*. Finally Mr. Logan called the camper's mother.

Back in our cabin, Billy packed his old gray suitcase with immense relief and waited, staring at the bare pine ceiling.

After the boy had asked to look at my watch for the eleventh time, we got word that his mother was down in the parking lot. I carried the heavy suitcase, and Billy skipped along ahead of me. Having seen the light come on in the kid's eyes, I expected some warm, loving woman to jump out of the car and run up to embrace her youngster. But as we left the treed path and walked toward the dusty Packard, a sloppily dressed, glum-faced matron strolled around back to open up the trunk. She gave her son a casual, graceless greeting. I waited in vain for some little show of affection to warm the woman's tepid exterior.

But Billy didn't seem to mind. She had come. In the twinkling of an eye he had returned from a dark, alien land to home sweet home. The first sighting of his mother had done it. He rested content in her ungainly presence.

The woman bid me a gruff good day and drove off. Billy was too preoccupied with his rescue to wave back at me through the rear window.

I haven't been able to forget the face of that blissful boy in the droopy Packard, or the way he placed all his security and happiness in the lap of a mother who seemed so utterly unattractive. The bare filial tie that riveted him to her side seemed to have the out-of-proportion power of an atomic bond.

As we grow older we forget how overwhelming something like homesickness can be. Maybe we've forgotten the time on a crowded sidewalk when

Mama's skirt slipped from our grasp and suddenly we looked around and she was gone—forever. How quickly we descended into terror. One can only compare it to the shock of an astronaut walking in space, who discovers that something has severed his or her cord to the space capsule.

Billy's experience of being so lost and so found gave me, quite unexpectedly, a glimpse of Christ and His intense love. Usually I picture Jesus as our elder brother or father. But that day he seemed, in a sense, very much like Billy, the devoted son.

Christ's longing for the citizens of our indifferent planet is elemental and inexplicable. We have little in us to attract His devotion. Our love is fickle and shallow. It doesn't even nudge the scale when compared with Christ's self-sacrificing regard.

Yet Jesus behaves as if His security is tied up with ours. He is restless when we wander and agonizes over our separation from Him. Endlessly He pleads for reunion. Christ did not consider heaven a place to be cherished while we were lost. Instead, He gave up His favored place in Paradise to come and live among those with stunted affections.

Billy's homesickness was acute because he was not yet self-contained. He hadn't gone through the adolescent struggle to become a truly separate individual. His identity still very much centered in his mother's.

The wonder is that God, the self-existent one, should feel an even greater homesickness for the guilty who have cut themselves off from Him. Our Lord has all the security and identity He could ever need. Yet He still makes Himself known primarily though His patient, persistent longing for us.

All my logic couldn't turn Billy from his single-minded desire for home. Neither did the camp director's authority carry any weight. None of the delights of summer camp we presented to him could get through the loneliness in his heart.

Fortunately for us, Christ demonstrated a single-minded purpose in the plan of salvation He unfolds in history. He is determined to break through all the obstacles. All human atrocities couldn't change His purpose. Thousands of years of Hebrew ambivalence couldn't deter Him, nor could the unfaithfulness of His disciples or even the defiant mockery around the cross of those He had come to save.

For a moment, standing on the gravel road of our camp, freckle-faced Billy filled me with wonder. I saw the self-existent One painfully homesick for the unlovely and unlovable ones who cut themselves off from Him. I realized His is a longing that nothing can turn aside.

And I found in Christ's homesickness for me a space in which to seek intimacy with Him. His inexplicable love is the place where my heart deepens. He has adopted me as a cherished relative, and that bare filial bond has great power.

Chapter Five

Step Past the Turkey

When I was quite young I somehow got it into my head that people-eating chickens ravaged the world. I suppose it started with the angry hen. Our paths crossed in Veracruz, Mexico, where my family was vacationing. I'm still not sure what set her off. But somehow, I had offended the egg layer, and she tore after me, chasing me around our 1957 Ford station wagon, her wings thrashing. Screaming in terror, I ran around and around the car until someone finally shooed the beast off.

The experience scarred me for life, of course. I developed an enormous fear of chickens. Only chickens. Snakes were no problem. Who knew what awesome powers lay just under those chicken feathers? And those hideous little heads, always pecking at the ground—as if to nail down your feet. I was deathly afraid of touching them.

Later I learned that many human beings share irrational fears. They can't help thinking that some slimy reptile will creep up through the toilet and attack them. But I was alone among humanity. I had to continually check for the aquatic rooster I was sure would someday emerge from the plumbing as I sat.

Various things I learned about life in the fourth and fifth grades gave me the impression that people-eating chickens are exceedingly rare on the earth. In a way, it disappointed me. Having distinct enemies does provide a certain kind of comfort.

But before I learned this, I had to go through a test of manhood. It happened during one of my mother's visits to a fellow church member just outside of Medellín, Colombia. The family was dirt-poor. As we approached, I could see that their home was a shack. And then I spotted the monster guarding their dilapidated gate: an enormous turkey. If chickens seemed lethal to me, you can imagine how this beast appeared, with that red thing hanging from his neck like some misplaced organ. At the gate it lurked just out of the way, but obviously waited for me.

Mother called out a greeting. Although I tried not to look at the turkey, its bug eyes and curved beak seemed to tower above us. A half-dozen half-naked children scurried out of the shack, followed by the mother, who beamed at us.

Mom pulled on my hand. The path lay before us, straight ahead to the house. It was time to go through the gate, a passage through purgatory.

And I made it. Swallowing hard, I just took a few steps. While the turkey seemed to gaze at me with some disdain, it did not attack. It didn't even follow us.

The straight dirt path that led to that shack has burned itself in my memory. Because that's what I was staring at hard as I went through the gate. Although a frightening strip of dirt at the time, long afterward that path has come to represent something quite wonderful.

My mother intended for me to meet the family for a special reason. She wanted me to know what giving is all about. I remember the floor of the house because it didn't have one—at least not one I was used to. The earth itself, packed down over time and swept smooth, had become their floor. And the shack had nothing inside it—nothing like the furniture in our living room. Just a few shelves with some pots and some mats leaning against the wall.

It was the first time I realized what poverty was. I saw that there were children in the world who were just like me, but who led vastly different lives. Yet they were the same kids who came to our Sabbath school and put their coins in the back of the little offering elephant. And as Mother later reminded me, this was the woman who brought an offering of some kind to church, wrapped in a bandanna, every week without fail. Mother explained that she and her family considered it a joy, a privilege, to give.

I don't remember all that she told me. But I do remember that path leading straight out of their shack to Sabbath school. And it has seemed to me a glorious little path, something that made the life of the dispossessed honorable and good.

They just did it—they just gave. It wasn't because they had some great insight on the principles of stewardship or particular vision for how the church could move forward with the right funds. They just did it because it was the right thing to do. What Paul said of Macedonian believers applied to them: "Their extreme poverty welled up in rich generosity" (2 Cor. 8:2). That Colombian family put their possessions on the line. No hesitation. No worries about tomorrow. No fear.

They just walked past the turkey.

MEANWHILE, BACK AT THE MALL . . .

In the years since then, that straight dirt path has blurred considerably in my mind. I now find myself in quite different circumstances. I have a house in the suburbs, with a monthly mortgage payment, and a teenage daughter who seems forever drawn to the mall.

My teenage son wants a new skateboard. You can't just walk in and buy the thing. No, in the "real" skate shop my son patronizes, you have to purchase it piece by piece—from bolt to bearing to kingpin to grip tape. When the clerk takes several plastic wheels from behind the counter for Jason to look over, I get the uneasy feeling we're inspecting diamonds. After the salesman adds up the total, it confirms my suspicion.

Giving to God isn't so simple anymore. In college I used to be able to turn up my nose at "money-grubbing businesspeople." It was easy to talk about the evils of materialism because I had no bills to pay. Now I'm grubbing along with everybody else. Trying to get something put away so we can get a new car. Trying to nudge up my script fees. Trying to widen my client base.

When my wife and I first married and lived on a shoestring, we seemed to be thanking God constantly. He was always coming through in the nick of time. We had to trust Him to provide for us—even necessities. It was an adventure. We were thankful for the furniture that came trickling in to our apartment from the most unexpected places. Each couch or coffee table told an edifying story.

Now I have a real job. And all the furniture in our Dutch Haven home must match, of course. No more junk. The living room looks nice, but it doesn't have much of a story to tell us.

Every time I pass the banners flying above model homes in a new tract I want to go in and check things out. I want a newer house, with those nice bronze bathroom fixtures, that stylish tile in the foyer, those polished granite kitchen counters.

At middle age financial security no longer sounds like a dirty phrase. I understand it completely. The tread of materialism is a sound I can hear clearly—and it's gaining on me.

It's not that I'm going to run off to Wall Street tomorrow in search of instant riches. While I have no desire to give up my faith, I do feel it stagnating. The ordinary grind of trying to make a buck seems to be numbing me bit by bit, day by day. Life focuses more on getting through the hassles and less on getting through to God. After I arrive home, I'm more apt to collapse by the TV than to find renewal in the Word.

Perhaps, like me, you find that religious life keeps eroding away to a minimum. You still go to church, still try to have worship with the kids once in a while, and still try to act decently. But it's like a subsistence diet—just enough to keep you alive.

I want somehow to recapture the devotion of that impoverished family in Colombia; I want to be moved by the generous Spirit that motivated them.

But when I turn to Scripture for a way out of my spiritual inertia, I don't find any magic formula. No incantation to break the spell. Instead, I find straight-arrow admonitions:

"Turn from these worthless things to the living God" (Acts 14:15).

"Return, faithless people; I will cure you of backsliding" (Jer. 3:22).

"'Return to me,' declares the Lord Almighty, 'and I will return to you'" (Zech. 1:3).

While it's true that only God can ultimately cure our apathy, our slip-sliding away into the doldrums, He does ask us to make the decision to turn, to take a step in His direction. The plea to "turn" frequently pops up in the Bible and implies that there is something freeing in the initial gesture we make toward God.

When the prophet Micah attempted to pry Israel out of its suffocating religious routine and spiritual inertia, he suggested this simple alternative: "What does the Lord require of you? To act justly and to love mercy and to walk humbly with your God" (Micah 6:8).

Micah's message seems to me the spiritual equivalent of "Just Do It." Take a step. Act justly. Only God can create spiritual momentum, but He does want us to move off dead center.

DON'T JUST SIT THERE—DO SOMETHING!

One day, back when I clung tenaciously to my idea of people-eating chickens, my father took me out to someone's ranch in Colombia. Dad enjoyed buying and selling horses. I loved horses too, but discovered something quite different when we arrived at the place. Chickens. Hordes of them covered the gravel driveway where we parked. Dad hopped out and strode over to greet the rancher—walking right through the bobbing carpet of ravenous beasts—then motioned for me to come.

Fortunately he had sort of cleared a path, and I gingerly made my way to him, eyeing all those hideous little heads pecking furiously at the gravel. But as Dad talked business, the chickens began closing in around us until we were a little human island in the midst of the evil creatures. Although I'm sure there were only a couple hundred of them, to my young mind they seemed to stretch from horizon to horizon. I didn't think I'd ever get out alive.

Dad kept talking about horses, and I kept praying for Moses to come down and part the sea of chickens for me. After visiting at length, the two adults shook hands, and Dad put his palm on my shoulder, turning me toward our car. I gulped. He wanted me to wade through the writhing field of beaks and feathers, every one of them clucking about how I had offended their sister hen years before.

In my heart I wanted Dad to carry me out, but was a couple years too old for that and unable to admit my shameful chicken dread. So I took a step. It wasn't a very big step, but the chicken sea parted. The deadly creatures started moving out of the way. Following a straight line, with Dad beside me, I took another step—and they obligingly pecked somewhere else.

I lost my terror of chickens some time ago and am now able to live with them in peace on the same planet. But that step I took has come back to teach me a lesson. It convicts me and unites with the voices of the prophets: "Turn."

Yes, I'm surrounded by a materialistic culture that suffocates spiritual life and isolates faith. The carnal values do seem to get all the prime time, all the blockbusters, all the magazine spreads. But the prophets tell me something about spiritual survival in that kind of environment. Moaning and groaning about all the bad things out there, I can keep looking at the vast sea of chickens, keep waiting passively for God to do something. Or I can take a step. Act justly. Walk humbly. Just do something positive.

The prophetic call to "turn" highlights the liberating power of simple, affirmative acts. Sometimes we do everything else but that. We read wonderful books about prayer or underline great biblical passages on it. Perhaps we attend seminars on prayer. But do we really pray? Great things start happening only when we actually do it.

Or we might read wonderful books on witnessing and memorize the New Testament strategy for successful outreach. We talk about witnessing and participate in events designed to stimulate it. But do we actually talk to someone about Jesus?

Some of us read books about overcoming past scars and forgiving those who've hurt us. Discussing and planning it, filtering our emotions and retracing the labyrinth of our dysfunction, we revisit the pain one more time. But what about that last step? Actually forgiving?

It's good that believers have come to understand a lot more about how we get stuck in unhealthy behaviors. Helping people through the process of recovery and the process of healing is beneficial. But no matter what kind of program you're in, whether it has 12 steps or 30, the last step is always the same. You have to do the right thing.

Pretending that "willpower has nothing to do with it," we can comfort each other with the sentiment that "just trying hard doesn't work." But at some point all of us have to take that step—we have to walk past the turkey. We can't think our way past it or feel our way past it—we have to "just do it." Each of us has to experience the liberating power of an affirmative act. "Do not merely listen to the word. . . . Do what it says" (James 1:22).

Micah's words have struck me in my present predicament. They relate to the malaise of materialism. Instead of just moaning about those model home banners that keep flagging me down, instead of just lamenting about how spiritually numbing the mall can be, I need to take a step in the opposite direction.

GOD ON THE LIVING ROOM WALL

During a church service I listened as an interesting couple talked about how they'd met because he'd called a wrong number. He was a Middle Eastern businessman and she a California yuppie. They said God had brought them together. I wondered what on earth for.

Then Shaker and Vicki Rezk began to talk about their ministry in Egypt. It sounded fascinating. Could it be that they were actually winning Muslims to Christ on a regular basis?

A church friend beside me was the first to get excited and suggested that God might be telling us something. The couple depended on individual supporters. I, however, had to work my way through several layers of "financial security." I was already sending money to a sponsored child in Brazil, to a Bible translator in Cameroon, and to a missionary in Thailand. I figured I was covering the bases. And those present monthly donations already maxed out what I had committed myself to.

It was, in fact, all quite painless. After receiving a script or royalty check I would send 10 percent of the amount to one of the ministries. It was a habit. Ten percent already belonged to the Lord. It was like paying a bill. No mess, no fuss, no annoying appeal letters.

But now this couple stood in front of me. They were reaching the Muslim world, something I had always made noises about Christians needing to do.

And so, nodding to my church friend, I walked past the turkey. It was just a little step, a modest pledge, but we responded.

A few months later Shaker and Vicki were in my living room showing us slides of their work. Most of the time when people come into your living room and show you pictures of their trip overseas, you pray for the projector bulb to burn out. But this was different.

I was witnessing a small revolution. God was building a church out of thin air through Shaker's ministry in his hometown, a place where Christian evangelists languished in barbaric jails, where the indigenous Coptic believers feared to make any waves lest they bring on more persecution. Despite the danger, Shaker went about his business, quietly talking friends and their families into the kingdom.

"Oh, yes," Shaker said, pointing to a slide, "the man up there on the edge of the field—he used to be a hit man."

"A what?"

"He used to break people's limbs for money. He was so good that a terrorist organization wanted to recruit him."

The man, Mahmed, stood on our living room wall, beaming—a dedicated follower of Christ.

Shaker talked about remarkable transformations with a quiet, unassuming manner. I could tell his life wasn't filled with distractions. He was focused on sharing Christ, just doing it. He has no master plan, no sophisticated resources, no formula for reaching Muslims. Instead, he just meets people, and they go and have some tea together and talk. No one would mistake him for a firebrand. And yet he's turning the religious universe upside down for more and more people of his Muslim town.

Vicki and Shaker's slides had nothing extraordinary about them. Many were washed out or out of focus. You could barely make out Shaker in a restaurant with a friend. Vicki at an orphanage. The couple leading their donkey through the streets.

But I had suddenly become part of something miraculous. I wasn't waiting around for God to do something great in my complacent, comfortable suburb. Instead, I'd simply taken a little step forward. And boom! There God was on our living room wall. Giving was no longer a reflex action. This couple had made it an act of the will.

Act justly. One affirmative act started to break the spell of "Absolutely nothing is happening in my life." I was walking down that dirt path that led from the shack straight to Sabbath school, clutching my offering in my hand, breathing in the Spirit of giving that awakens us from our mall-to-mall slumber.

It's these small gestures, these small steps, that set us off on the journey toward intimacy with God. He uses them to break through our spiritual inertia, then magnifies their effect.

In the sections that follow, we'll look at the various ways in which God deepens our hearts to create room for intimacy. So far we've covered the groundwork for everything that follows. We need to make sure that hidden guilt isn't an obstacle—so we clear away the clutter in honest confession before God. To erase insecurity as an obstacle, we begin to build a sense of self that relates to a separate, holy, loving God. And we must overcome spiritual inertia by responding in some way to God.

The good news is that God amplifies our small steps into spiritual breakthroughs. Although we decide to turn, it's God who wills and acts inside us for His good purpose (Phil. 2:13). We may reach out in love, but it's God who pours out His affection abundantly into our hearts (Rom. 5:5). And we may stretch in faith, but God does "immeasurably more than all we ask or imagine, according to his power that is at work within us" (Eph. 3:20).

He's the one who is eager to deepen our hearts, the one who most longs for intimacy.

Part Three

Relationships
That Deepen Our Hearts

Chapter Six

A Photograph in Jerusalem

As we approached the hills west of Jerusalem, the tour guide in our bus grabbed his microphone and lectured, "Do you know why there are so many stones on the side of this road? We think of them as the burdens which pilgrims have carried all their lives—the longing to visit this holy city. When the pilgrims finally reach the crest of these hills, they drop their burden—they know their lifelong dream is about to come true. Your lifelong dream is about to come true too."

Night had settled over the city, and heavy rains poured down. We couldn't see much out the windows except a cluster of lights that spread out on hills as nondescript as those of any town. But I wasn't really disappointed. It was a sign, I told myself. Coming to the Holy Land has to be an exercise of the imagination—you have to cooperate with the ruins and barren landscape in order to see it the way it once was.

The next day we walked through narrow streets and a foggy drizzle toward an excavation site—the basement of a house that probably burned when Titus razed Jerusalem in A.D. 70. A pattern of half-buried stones suggested the skeleton of a lavish mansion where Caiaphas probably partied.

Then they told us we were going to the upper room. I pictured Jesus reclining with the twelve, rising up to retrieve the towel and basin, washing away pride and animosity, breaking bread and wine, and seeing His own body given up as the ultimate sacrifice. Yes, you can't help it—you want to walk where Jesus walked.

We climbed a stairway, declined the cheesy Last Supper fans several boys tried to sell us, and entered an empty hall. The Crusaders had built in the arched ceiling. We sang "My Jesus, I Love Thee" along the cracked, poorly painted walls. I looked around at the other faces singing. Among them were Darryl and Humberto. Darryl, a friend who'd come from a background of dysfunction and legalism, wanted to celebrate the gospel that had rescued him—and do it on holy ground. And Humberto Noble Alexander, a courageous Cuban pastor who'd suffered greatly in Castro's prisons, was celebrating his new unhindered ministry in the United States. I kept thinking that I needed to get to know these two people better. But I was too preoccupied with the setting to really enjoy our voices echoing the faith together. I couldn't get past the fact that the place was just a room and not the sacred past. Its main claim to authenticity was that it occupied a second story and no one was living there at the time.

At the Western Wall I did see Jewish people touching the past as they inserted their prayers on slips of paper into the seams of the great stones. It was the original foundation wall of Solomon's Temple . . . or was it Herod's Temple? Israeli soldiers in green fatigues, carrying assault rifles, eyed us all with profound suspicion, as their job dictated. Suddenly, just above us, the Muslim call to worship erupted from the mosque on the holy mount and rained down on the petitioners at the Western Wall. No wonder these people are always at each other's throats. The Holy Land has too much holy real estate crammed together. On the day we were there a group of pious men worshiping at the wall started throwing chairs in order to get the women praying and wailing to pipe down. Ambulances took a few away.

Jesus didn't seem to be in the neighborhood. But what about the Mount of Olives? I still had high hopes for that famous slope. Unfortunately, as we walked toward it through the Kidron Valley, we had to avoid the discarded appliances and rusting gasoline cans that litter the place. Arriving on top of the mount itself, we saw that it is cluttered with tombs, a dense ghetto of white stone slabs. The deceased are crowded together like sunbathers on Labor Day weekend. Tradition has the Resurrection beginning at this spot, and many have wanted to be first in line.

The Garden of Gethsemane, or remnant thereof, is nice. But of course, it has long been enclosed by a church. They've landscaped the ground around the gnarled roots of the olive trees and put in pretty flowers. The stone where Jesus supposedly prayed His heart out forms the nave of the church. You can get close and kneel, but in the muted light the stone appears covered by a heavy layer of makeup. Smooth and creamy, no blemishes. This is not the Son of God flinging Himself to the ground in anguish—it's incense and incantation.

Fruit venders crowd the Via Dolorosa. The Church of the Holy Sepulcher is vast and vaulted. It attempts to enshrine both the site of the Crucifixion and the site of Jesus' tomb. Both in one building? That sort of miniaturizes things. I wanted Calvary to be some great summit, jagged against the sky, with plenty of room for the Crucifixion as spectacle, and space for all the extras.

But now Mount Calvary lies under glass. I peered down at it through a clear plastic floor, which priests in stocking feet keep polished. It was the same Max Factor rock, all creamy and nice. The space around it was dense with candles, crucifixes, and icons. Gold and silver gleamed everywhere. I felt like I was in some quaint department store. Standing there gawking at all the goods, I couldn't imagine anything more removed from the violent drama of that providential execution. It would be easier to think of Calvary on the hill in back of my house.

During the long bus rides between sites I occasionally looked over at Darryl and Humberto, thinking we should talk more. But I kept nodding off because of jet lag. Anyway, we were always rushing around from one significant historical site to another. I still wanted to touch something holy. Maybe I'd find it outside of Jerusalem.

Bethlehem sounded promising. I hoped we might even catch a glimpse of shepherds tending flocks on the hills. Something to take us back, something to make us feel we were close to a world Jesus inhabited.

What greeted us in the streets of Bethlehem was angry graffiti, steel grates, and rolled-down gates. The Arab residents had gone on strike, closing all the stores to protest something the Israelis had done. The guides told us to keep quiet as we rode to the Church of the Nativity so the bus wouldn't become the object of a political statement (i.e., get stoned).

The church seemed like another musty museum to me. The Shrine of the

Nativity, designated as the place where Mary laid Baby Jesus, occupied the basement. The manger has been decorated with all the art that centuries of adoration and three competing religious traditions can muster. It has everything but pulsating neon lights. Failing to enter into the spirit of the shrine, I saw only gaudy trinkets and wondered how cows or donkeys could ever get anywhere near the place.

It didn't get any better up in Nazareth. The neighborhood has changed drastically since Jesus moved out. I could catch only asphalt, diesel fumes, and lax zoning laws, and felt ever more removed from the places where Jesus walked.

But I tried to get close. Skipping rocks on the Sea of Galilee, I looked out on the flat, gray water and tried to see Jesus telling His disciples where to fish. Walking off by myself on a green slope above the lake, I tried to hear the Sermon on the Mount.

A person can use his or her imagination, but there's so little help. The religious quotation marks around every holy site tend to obliterate the little authenticity left. In Capernaum a grid of black stones mark out the foundations of houses that stood in Jesus' time. One of them may have been Peter's. They found Christian inscriptions on a wall.

But of course, they've built a church on top of the excavation. Lay down the gold, silver, and glass. Light the candles. Put on the makeup. We get farther than ever from touching—we're just commemorating.

But what did I expect? Maybe I was trying too hard. Poking about on the desolate road down to Jericho, I almost expected to find carved on rock: "The Good Samaritan Was Here." But I saw no messages anywhere. After all, you can only remember. You can't re-create.

RECAPTURING THE GLORY DAYS

My missed experience in the Holy Land made me think a lot about coming so close, yet remaining so far. Maybe a lot of us have been looking for intimacy in all the wrong places.

Many times our efforts to recapture a sense of closeness with God involve trying to get back to a certain place. We have our own version of the Holy Land, in which certain wonderful experiences happened. Maybe it was the site of a retreat, a particular church, or a certain campus. We want to travel back to the spawning ground of spiritual intimacy, put our hands on it, and compress that place into some kind of souvenir. Perhaps we want to be able to place it in a drawer so we can take it out whenever we want to feel the wonder again.

To those who really long for intimacy, it's hard to shake this romantic notion of rediscovering the magic of place. If we could just touch it again, just walk into that wonderful worship service once again, God would seem powerfully close. Or if we could just hear that dynamic pastor once more, he or she would sweep us into intimacy with Christ.

But when we do try to go back, we usually find we're just commemorating. It's not the same. We can't re-create that wonderful experience. As soon as we put religious quotation marks around intimacy, it tends to fade away. The souvenirs we pick up don't really pack the same punch.

It's tempting to keep looking for intimacy in some exotic experience, in the pilgrimage back to that faraway place. Things on the distant horizon seem to pull at us more deeply. But what we're looking for may be much closer at hand. Maybe it's so familiar we've been looking right through it.

RIGHT BEFORE OUR EYES

After quite a few groggy bus rides and musty museums I finally found what I was looking for in the Holy Land. It happened in the countryside south of Jerusalem, in a dry creekbed, or wadi, between two hills. One, a gentle slope, had been where the Philistine army once lined up in battle formation for an all-out assault. The other, a steeper bluff, protected the Israelite soldiers as they quaked in their sandals.

At the site of this famous David-and-Goliath confrontation we tourists/pilgrims busied ourselves in the creekbed, each choosing five stones that looked about right, which we could then take back home. I decided it would be a good time to take a picture of Darryl and Humberto, my two companions on the tour. We joked around while I posed Darryl, who is very tall, as Goliath lifting a stick and lumbering through the creekbed. Humberto, who is rather short, had a stone in his hand, aimed at Darryl's forehead.

We were, of course, re-creating that providential encounter in which David felled the warrior giant. But as Darryl and Humberto posed good-naturedly, something else hit me right between the eyes. Here was another miracle staring me in the face. Two of them, in fact. Who were those figures I was looking at through the camera? Who were those people who'd been riding with me on the bus hour after hour as we fought off jet lag in between stops at holy places?

They were acts of God.

SEEING THE FACE OF GOD'S LOVE

Darryl had grown up under the influence of an abusive father, a man who tormented his children to such an extent that Darryl's fragile younger brother had to be committed to an institution. During his childhood Darryl had experienced enough pain and anger to handicap him for life. Under the influence of his father's fanatical religion, he had compressed all his emotional devastation within an extremely strict religious life. He had to serve God with a vengeance—getting rid of everything pleasurable in his life, trying to become worthy of divine favor. No letting up, no letting go.

The man shaking a stick in that creekbed had every reason to become an abusive parent himself. His heart should have been as desolate as the Judean desert. What resources could he possibly draw upon? All he knew of fatherhood was a terrible distortion. Darryl often told me he would have been far better off as an orphan.

But grace entered his life. The first big breakthrough came via the psalms of the shepherd boy who'd also been in this creekbed. One day when Darryl was reading his Bible (obsessively), a few verses suddenly opened up for him a radically different picture of God. God as a Father who has compassion on His children. A Father of the fatherless. Someone who cares for us even if our human parents forsake us.

Here wasn't an endlessly demanding deity, but Someone just the opposite of his human father. Darryl kept looking and began to discover grace, justification by faith, and acceptance in Christ. The force of the gospel overwhelmed him. He found a place to start over again, ground he could stand on and not have to defend himself continually, to continually struggle to be worthy.

Darryl plunged into the gospel like a thirsty nomad diving into the pool of an oasis. He soaked it up. It sunk in deep. And God began to bear fruit in a spiritual desert.

I'd seen it happen. My kids grew up with Darryl's. I always liked watching my friend with his two children. He has such a gracious way of disarming little arguments. His good humor eases the kids through their missteps. Darryl doesn't have to raise a stick—he wins them over to goodness.

It continued that way as his kids and mine reached their teenage years. Darryl has been consistent and sensitive, someone his boy and girl have always been able to cling to.

I saw it at the cat wedding. The kids, who love felines, wanted to have a ceremony for a male and female who were becoming intimate in the closet. Darryl waited at the altar as the four-footed couple followed bits of cat food down an aisle in the living room. And in the midst of the fun, he was able to share very winsomely some truths about sex and fidelity for his teenagers.

I saw it when Darryl's son dyed his hair an unearthly orange. The boy was stretching against tradition and distancing himself from conventional religion. But Darryl didn't panic or try to hang on by force. He let his son wander a bit, always watching to make sure he stayed within certain boundaries.

And I saw it in the way Darryl guided his daughter through the early years of high school. She was the more insecure of the two children, and when the family moved across country, she worried a lot about making new friends. But Darryl built her confidence step by step, day by day, always telling her how lovely she was in his eyes. And his daughter blossomed into a confident young woman. She will never have to chase after some guy in order to get self-esteem.

Staring at Darryl as he clowned in the creekbed, making threatening gestures, I couldn't help feeling awed by the miracle. This man once had to cower in his bed at night, listening to his father's vicious abuse raining down on him. But his own kids have grown up secure, nestled against the rock of fatherly love.

The heavenly Father has reproduced Himself. He has become flesh and is dwelling among us. Darryl had no business growing up normal, much less becoming a great father. But God disrupted the inevitable cycle. Out of an angry, bitter wasteland, a compassionate father blossomed and bore fruit.

I began to feel that maybe this dusty creekbed was indeed holy ground.

SEEING THE FACE OF GOD'S JOY

And what about the little guy posing among the white stones, aiming at the giant? David wasn't the only underdog to take a courageous stand in the name of God. Here in the flesh, in front of my eyes, was another giant slayer, Humberto Noble Alexander.

Throughout his incarceration, the Goliath of Communist thought control worked overtime to eliminate any vestiges of faith among political prisoners. But Humberto managed to lead a vibrant and growing underground church in the cell blocks. He later told me that those years spent in a brutal prison were the most fruitful and rewarding of his whole life.

During one particularly brutal crackdown on those involved in religious activities, Humberto led his men in a hunger strike to protest the abuse. Prison officials hung tough, and the congregation dwindled to about 30.

One evening as the men gathered to worship, Humberto noticed a guard in the sniper's cage counting the number of prisoners in attendance. The group had just finished singing "Trust and Obey" when a soldier burst into the room. "All you cult members, get out here and line up!" he ordered.

Everyone glanced at each other and then down at the floor. They knew what was coming: a trip to the isolation cells for punishment. Humberto led the way out into the courtyard. The soldier walked down the line of prisoners and then announced, "There are only 20 of you here. I counted 30 in there. Where are the other 10?"

Humberto tried to avoid the soldier's gaze. He was praying for strength to endure the severe beating he would get as the group's leader. Neither he nor anyone else in the line wanted to betray the 10 men who had slipped away.

The soldier continued shouting for the names of the missing men. By this time many other prisoners had gathered in the courtyard to watch. Finally the guard waved his rifle and declared, "If those 10 inmates don't appear immediately, I'm going to punish the entire cellblock."

Now Humberto had a serious problem. While no one wanted to betray a fellow prisoner, neither did any inmate, especially a nonreligious one, want to submit to a flogging because someone else broke the rules.

Humberto kept praying. Suddenly a prisoner who had never attended his meetings or shown any interest in Christianity stepped forward. "I am one of the 30 men," he said.

Then a second inmate, also not part of the congregation, stepped over to join the group. Several others followed. Before Humberto could quite grasp what was going on, more than 50 additional prisoners declared that they had attended the meeting.

The soldier's face reddened. Many of the prison's isolation cells were already occupied. They didn't have enough room for all the additional people. Furious and frustrated, the man stomped off to see his superior officer—and never returned.

After this incident, many of those who had stepped forward to declare a new allegiance began attending services. And they stayed. Humberto's congregation quickly tripled. They were men who had come under the influence of a believer who consistently stood against Goliath. The giant had stumbled again. Many more human beings had slipped into the safety of God's kingdom.

Standing in that dry creekbed in Israel, I felt again the force of Humberto's cheerful courage. In watching him wield his stone against Darryl, I seemed to have found holy ground.

THE FACE OF CHRIST . . . CLOSER THAN WE THINK

Throughout the tour I'd been trying to stick my shoes in Jesus' footsteps, seeking to get close to Him by visiting places where He had once performed miracles. I wanted to feel His presence in special places. But all the time He was beckoning to me in the persons of two friends. All the time real intimacy was as close as their faces. God was saying, "Look what I've done. Do you see My Fatherhood in this tall, gangly man who nurtured two fragile human beings into healthy youth? Do you feel My love in the gentle way he shares his firm convictions? And can you sense My irrepressible joy in the face of this Cuban pastor? You can't see traces of martyrdom in his eyes—only see a faith as bold and confident as David's—'Let's go out and slay the giant.' Can you see in him the fire of My passion to rescue the lost?"

God didn't keep Darryl and Humberto under glass. They didn't appear holy only in candlelight, but were living testimonies of the wonder of a living Christ. And I wanted to be close to Him.

Christ did finally come very close to me on a stop near Gethsemane. We were walking down the Mount of Olives when we entered a modest olive grove. Nothing said "holy" there. A discarded, rusting washing machine suggested how much the neighbors thought of the place. Only a few humble trees hinted at the forest that had once covered the mountain.

But as I looked at Humberto and Darryl, it all came over me as I realized again who those people really were. I remembered that Darryl had told me he wanted to slip out of the hotel and spend the night out on Gethsemane, praying. "Wouldn't that be wonderful?" he said. For security reasons we weren't supposed to go wandering out in the dark. But Darryl wanted to pray where Jesus had prayed. He wanted to pray joyfully and exorcise the ghost of those very different nights of his boyhood.

Still dazed from jet lag and needing all the sleep I could get, I hadn't been too enthusiastic about the idea. But now, looking at Darryl against the olive grove, I realized he really could get inside Jesus' anguish. To him it wasn't just a place, just a commemoration. Gethsemane was right here and right now. My companion could taste the joy of that great deliverance when Jesus took on the weight of our pain and anger on His shoulders, when He took on all the cruelty and abuse and allowed it to crush out His life. Yes, how marvelous that rescue. I could see it in Darryl's intense expression, his restless hands, his awkward eagerness.

Well, it was too late for the all-nighter. The best I could do was get another picture. Asking someone to shoot the three of us against the olive trees, I stood between them, with tall Goliath on one side and short David on the other, and put my arms around them. I was grinning lightheartedly on the outside, but inside I was hugging the Lord Jesus Christ. I have never in my life been so proud of Him, never been so filled with wonder at His works. The photograph is quite ordinary—just three tourists in Jerusalem, smiling back at the camera in front of a low stone wall that borders the grove. But to me it will always speak eloquently of sacred ground. It reminds me there is no such thing as holy places, only holy faces.

Chapter Seven

Giving Our
Hearts a Voice

O ne summer my brother Dan decided that the grandchildren of Vernon and Clarenda Smith should have a reunion. Since we hadn't seen each other in a long time, we decided that just the cousins should get together, without the usual company of aunts and uncles and all the family baggage that accumulates over the years.

We congregated in San Antonio. All the kids I had played with at Grandmother Smith's house in Houston were now adults—some with families—and all were focused on their various careers. We had a lot of fun catching up on each other's lives. Paying our respects at the Alamo, we feasted at Mexican restaurants, visited the rowdy night spot where cousin Bett sings (and ended up throwing food at each other), rafted the Guadalupe River, and played charades back at the hotel.

A great time was had by all. But we were still just yuppies visiting old acquaintances until late one night, during a lull in charades, when cousin Debbie mentioned something about Grandmother. We should have invited her to come. She was, after all, the center of the family.

The turn in conversation led one cousin to bring up Grandmom's breakfasts: biscuits and gravy, grits, and scrambled eggs. And yes, the times we used to chase each other all through her house—except through the one forbidden room, the stylish parlor where she received formal guests.

Someone else remembered the green chair Granddad always sat in, watching a TV that hummed for a while before it came on. We recalled lazy, humid afternoons listening to his thunderous snoring as he napped. Each of us savored the memory of that deeply lined face, weathered by years as a roughneck out in the oil fields, his gravel-voiced laughter, and the smell of his pipe before he gave it up. Stories circulated about setting out with him in the predawn chill for fishing trips on the Brazos River.

We remembered all the houses Grandmom and Granddad had lived in and what it was like to drive up from a long distance, jump out of the car, and run into Grandmom's arms. I talked about flying out with my son Jason to see Granddad in the hospital. Dying of cancer, he had drifted in and out of consciousness. But for a moment, before passing from us, he had recognized the 4-year-old in my arms and reached out to grab his ankle. Jason still remembers Granddad's last words: "You little rascal."

The more we talked in that hotel room, the more we remembered. Granddad and Grandmom Smith were absent, but I doubt we'd ever felt their presence, their love for us, the force of their personalities, more strongly. And suddenly we'd become more than just former acquaintances with a bit of genealogy in common. Now we were family members, bound together by two colorful figures in our lives. Not wanting the moment to end, we continued reminiscing far into the night.

THE "COUSIN REUNION" OF BELIEVERS

When we come together in church as brothers and sisters in Christ, the idea is to have fellowship, a reunion in the Spirit. But what we end up with most of the time is the moral equivalent of paying our respects at the Alamo. We stand up and sit down and kneel together on cue and listen to nice speeches about God. Perhaps we play charades with other believers, acting out our devotion, making pious gestures. But all this rarely produces intimacy. Sometimes we're loneliest while sitting crowded together in the pew.

I've often noticed a dramatic difference between life in the pews and life in the foyer of a church. During the religious part of our fellowship—the sermon, in particular—the expressions of worshipers slowly reduce to dull stares. Shoulders sag, eyes glaze over. By the end of the service many of us must be roused from a stupor. But as soon as the organ recessional dies out and we step out into the foyer, our expressions dramatically transform. Everyone becomes animated. Faces completely expressionless a few seconds before now race through a spectrum of bright emotions. Sparkling eyes, lively gestures, and energetic voices fill the foyer.

But usually we're not talking about the sermon. It's not something that happens inside the church that turns our stupor into excitement. Instead, it's perfectly ordinary things: the weather, someone's new dress, a baby, something funny that happened that week, what the kids are doing these days. People are just happy about seeing each other and catching up. That creates a great deal of energy. And the electricity that keeps this interaction going is simply life in general.

Since I have witnessed this remarkable transformation between pew and foyer countless times, I've often thought: *Wouldn't it be wonderful if we could somehow combine the best of both worlds? What if we could combine the talk about God that goes on inside the sanctuary with the animated interaction that occurs just outside it? Is there any way that the acts of God commemorated in the pew can merge with the "real life" we share in the foyer?*

Something very much like this happened during that reunion in San Antonio. Our interaction focused around two central figures: our grandparents. But we weren't just making speeches, commemorating their good deeds—we were *reliving* them. We talked about the ordinary events, the stuff of life, that had bonded our hearts to theirs. Every anecdote added to the picture, and every story added texture to our memories.

These experiences were already inside each individual in that circle of cousins. They had been there, lying dormant for years. But we didn't taste them, didn't sense their power, until we shared the memories together. They had to be expressed openly. That's when the love of our grandparents became tangible to us.

Wonderful stories reside inside the believers in the foyer saying "Hello, nice day" or "How was your week?" These earthen vessels have treasures inside them. We've bumped into God here and there in our everyday lives. Each of us has encounters and anecdotes to tell. But all this doesn't really turn into fellowship unless we express it. Our memories have to find a voice. We have to find a way to stop the rush of activity—all the things we're supposed to be doing at the "cousin reunion" that is church—and just focus on the Central Figure in our lives.

I don't suggest that the foyer is the only place to do that. It's perfectly natural and healthy just to shoot the breeze with your friends after church. But if we are to help each other experience intimacy with God, then somewhere, somehow, sometime, we have to share the good memories. If *all* our interaction as believers happens within the safe boundaries of "Isn't it a lovely day?" then a lot of good material is going to waste away inside us. The most important part of life is slipping away while we're talking trivia.

The spiritual side of our experience needs to come out in the open. We must share it. It requires the animated voice, the vigorous gesture, the bright expressions of the foyer. That's one big way we taste and see that the Lord is good.

The writer of Hebrews gives us this classical exhortation regarding fellowship: "And let us consider how we may spur one another on toward love and good deeds. Let us not give up meeting together, . . . but let us encourage one another" (Heb. 10:24, 25). What kind of "meeting together" can this refer to? Surely not just a seat on the same pew. General talk about abstract principles is not an efficient way of stirring up others to active goodness. The most potent interaction is always specific, personal, and face-to-face.

CHANGING THE QUESTION

While working at a Christian language school in Japan I got tired of greeting the other teachers with the same old banalities every day. As we passed in the hallway, retrieved our lessons from the lounge, or chatted in between classes, our conversation was pleasant enough, but usually uninspiring. It seemed ironic. There we were, in an utterly secular society, trying to present the gospel through our Bible classes and evangelistic meetings, trying to help our Japanese friends see the light—and yet that light never seemed to flicker between us. If the gospel was indeed, as we presented it, the great answer for humanity, why did it echo so rarely in our own daily lives?

So I got together with a few buddies and we decided to replace our "Hey, how ya doin'?" "OK; nice day" routine with one simple question: "What did you learn today?" Many of us were trying to develop a consistent time of daily devotions, motivated by the goal of making Christianity real to people who drew a blank when someone mentioned the word "God." What if we tried to share something specific we'd discovered through our time in prayer and the Word? A few of us determined to ask the question each morning as our greeting and to wait for an answer.

That simple act sparked a chain reaction. People all over the school started talking about the real struggles and exciting discoveries in their lives. Soon everyone was joining in. The fact that we were asking each other about our spiritual experience "right now" helped a lot of us dig into the Word more in order to find something definite to share. Not only did we encourage others; we found that talking about some useful principle reinforced that truth in our own minds. We were helping each other grow, building each other up. That ethereal, pious word "fellowship" had found a place in the world of flesh and blood. We had a great time—and we changed our world. The teachers' lounge and hallways of our English school were never quite the same again.

REMEMBER THE WAY WE USED TO FEEL?

One of the experiences that motivated me to start writing this book was a conversation I had with a woman from church. She worked at a denominational headquarters and had lots of wonderful ideas about how to empower believers for ministry at the local church level. But when I asked her about her background, she said that she didn't feel as connected to God as she once did. Even when she'd drifted away from the church as a young woman, she still had a deep, emotional bond with the Lord. Her spiritual life had a freshness and innocence back then, but now . . .

"Do you feel kind of blah about God because you're dealing with religious matters all the time at work?" I asked.

"That's part of it," she answered. "But there's more. It's something like a long-term marriage. It has warmth and coziness and comfort in the relationship, but no fireworks."

The sound of resignation in her voice cut right through me. I couldn't stand the thought of anyone investing so many years in the Christian life yet coming away feeling so disconnected. It had to have fireworks of some kind, some kind of intimacy.

Then she said, "Think about it—do you know anyone our age who is really excited about God?"

That really set me back. At that moment I couldn't point to any middle-aged firebrands. More than that, I couldn't even see the possibility of recovering that fire. It was frightening.

Since that conversation I've thought a lot about why people become emotionally disconnected. And one question keeps popping up: Do people actually talk about what God is doing in their lives?

I think that's what forms the dividing line: the things we talk about. Spiritual life needs expression. Even when nothing much seems to be going on, even when we're stuck in a rut, God is active. He's around and has something up His sleeve. Talking about Him can get us off dead center.

Just speaking about what you *want* God to do in your life is a great start. Simply expressing those longings can help get them started. The important thing is to move beyond doctrinal debates and abstract discussions to conversation about something we feel.

Sometimes it seems that recapturing a sense of intimacy with God is like trying to recover the innocence and energy of youth. But then I turn around, and it's so close at hand—at my fingertips, on the tip of my tongue. It's a matter of expression. I need to stop settling for superficial exchanges and interrupt the endless flow of pleasantries with one good word, one good question such as "What did you learn today?"

One consistent thing unites the most important feelings in life: if we don't give them expression, they die. That's certainly true of love. I no longer buy the excuse "Well, I do love my [wife, children, God], but I just don't express it very well." Hogwash. Love that isn't expressed doesn't exist. We create it as we express it. Silent hearts always shrink. Always.

We produce intimacy by telling others how much the Central Figure in our lives means to us. That's how our hearts deepen. We find more room to love and be loved by God when we give our emotions a voice, when we taste and share them with other people.

In Ephesians Paul advertised being filled with the Spirit as an alternative to getting drunk on wine. And he proposed that the new wine of the Spirit should loosen our tongues, moving us past the usual bland chatter and toward creative expression: speaking psalms, hymns, and spiritual songs to each other and making music in our hearts to God, always giving thanks (Eph. 5:19, 20).

Philippians, Paul's great Prison Epistle of joy, has the apostle eager to start a chain reaction. "I am glad and rejoice with all of you. So you too should be glad and rejoice with me" (Phil. 2:17, 18). The joy in God we express together becomes much more than the sum of its parts.

Before Jesus descended into the ordeal of trial and crucifixion, He experienced one moment of glorious expression. Luke tells us that as the Master rode His donkey down the Mount of Olives toward Jerusalem, the crowd escorting Him "began joyfully to praise God in loud voices for all the miracles they had seen" (Luke 19:37). As His followers ecstatically threw down palm branches and even their own clothes before Him, Jesus at last saw a multitude celebrating His presence. The excitement spilled out of church into the foyer. People shouted what had before been only hopeful whispers.

Later at the Temple even children joined in the joyful noise. When officials frowned on what they considered an unseemly display, Jesus warned, "If they keep quiet, the stones will cry out" (verse 40). Jesus was saying that joy in God just has to come out. Like a force of nature, it must find expression. And if human hearts are too hard to join in the praises, then the rocks themselves will have to turn into a chorus.

Today we can become part of that triumphal procession because we can still celebrate this Central Personality in our lives. He's still doing wonderful things. And wonderful things happen when we proclaim Him with animated voice, vigorous gesture, and bright expression. When we're willing to bear witness, God can even create something out of nothing.

MISSIONARY WITHOUT A CAUSE

Perry had no business being a missionary and he knew it. He didn't have a clue as to why he was stuck in Japan, trying to teach the Bible to students at an English language school. When the kindly dean at his Canadian college had suggested that he take a year off for service overseas, Perry'd had every intention of telling him no. He had no interest in religion. But the answer somehow came out yes.

The 20-year-old knew that his lifestyle bore only a casual resemblance to the message he had to present before eager Japanese college students and businesspeople. His amorous adventures at the Christian college he'd attended had on more than one occasion almost gotten him kicked out. And he didn't feel at all repentant. Fortunately, however, he'd absorbed enough Bible instruction as a kid to be able to repeat the usual verities and stories. After a while he even found himself presenting them with some enthusiasm. Still, he felt anguish inside as his double life took its toll.

One evening he was visiting with a group in a student's home, chatting pleasantly, drinking tea and snacking on rice crackers. At 8:00 the host nodded to Perry. Everyone stopped talking, got out their Bibles, and looked at him. He was supposed to teach them, but hadn't prepared! Suddenly the usually articulate young man found himself with absolutely nothing to say. He had nothing to give straight from the heart.

Racking his brain, he recalled a Scripture promise about the Lord giving a person the right words when brought before tribunals. Uttering a quick, desperate prayer to the God he'd been keeping at arm's length, he opened his mouth. The story of the prodigal son started coming out. Perry relaxed, figuring he might be able to wing it since it was one of the most familiar Bible stories in the world.

But as he described the father's persistent love for his ungrateful, profligate son, something happened to him. The words began to really register. As Perry told the smiling, nodding faces around him how marvelous God's unconditional love for us really is, that fact began to sink in to his own life. His own exposition ambushed him. He was hearing it all as if it were new.

After his talk Perry managed with some difficulty to bid polite good nights to everyone, then rushed home to his apartment. Falling beside his bed, overwhelmed by grace, he sobbed out his heartfelt repentance. Perry saw as clearly as a person can that God didn't just love the whole world—He loved this lone pseudomissionary kneeling in a darkened room. How could he have not realized it before? His tears welled up into a new spiritual life.

I knew Perry in Japan as an exuberant, thoughtful friend. He never tired of affirming that God had converted him as he was trying to speak things he didn't believe. His reluctant confession found its way into his heart—and unexpectedly deepened it. Suddenly it had room for intimacy with the God who had pursued him for so long.

Chapter Eight

Giving Ourselves Away

A split second at Borchard Community Park—that's all it was. A semistranger passing by. But it later caught me in the solar plexus.

Our church was having a thirtieth anniversary shindig at the park, with lots of old friends and rows of casseroles. I was walking in with my token salad-in-a-bag from Hughes market when the man went by.

I don't remember the name. But the face, yes. The chronically unshaven look, the slack jaw, the still intelligent eyes. I had met him one Thursday night when it was my turn to stay overnight at the homeless shelter. He was different from most of the residents, who were firmly, if secretly, attached either to the bottle or to their emotional disturbances. The man walked the streets eight hours a day, looking for work, facing one rejection after another.

One day the bottom had fallen out of his life: a pink slip followed quickly by his wife's goodbye. Emotionally devastated, he'd crashed through the solid middle-class like a wrecking ball—and landed in the basement.

That day I faced him again, a beaten figure trudging right by me and my Hughes salad. And I didn't say a word, even though his face revealed a loneliness that penetrated to the bone. I didn't stop, didn't miss a step.

We had an obscene amount of food that day for the big occasion. All the wonderful church women—and a few men—brought their best dishes. They had to lay it out in two separate lines. Jell-O salads jiggling with bananas, nuts, and peaches. Scalloped potatoes and broccoli and cheese dishes that melted in your mouth. Taco salads, pasta salads, bean combos, and a welter of entrées. Cookies and cake. Much would be carted home afterward.

But none of it would touch this semistranger. I had made a beeline past him toward my friends, the cool guys who can talk both sports and theology. Eagerly I prepared to go through my usual after-church potluck ritual of seeing how much food I can stack on one flimsy paper plate without grossing the women out.

Afterward I remembered that I'd seen the man one other time at the library where I go to do research. He was nodding off to sleep, so I'd told myself that he didn't want to be disturbed and had passed by. Besides, I figured, I had to get busy and dig up stories about how Christ touches and transforms human lives.

YOU STICK TO YOUR LIFE, AND I'LL STICK TO MINE

That's what scares me these days—it's so easy to walk on by. I don't even feel that yank of conscience, the pull of duty. Saying no is so easy. Countless qualifications cushion the basic instinct to do good.

I've got my boundaries, knowing where I mow the grass and where I don't, where the neighbor's curb problem ends and mine begins. As time passes, I find that my circle of acquaintances naturally gets more and more Christian. Even among believers I start to have definite preferences. I know exactly whom I like to hang out with and whom I don't. As an adult I don't have to deal with jerks or with people who come to the door or call on the phone. I don't have to put up with anything I don't want to.

It's good, of course, to have the kind of boundaries that keep other people from abusing or manipulating you. But I see other kinds of boundaries criss-crossing that land of "nothing is happening in my life." Those boundaries mark off lifestyle zones, zones of comfort. You naturally want to keep all the hassles on the other side. And before you know it, your zone of comfort gets a moat around it. You find yourself walking without a twitch past the homeless semistranger.

I could have made a difference that day. It wasn't just the food spread out on our picnic tables in abundance that was begging to be shared—it was the fellowship. I had joyful human contact coming out of my ears, but I couldn't spare any for this man in the crumpled clothes who was dying for a crumb.

I still can't shake the look on that homeless semistranger's face. That day in the park, it became painfully clear that the biggest force shrinking my religion was my own insulation, my own walls.

Love is the stuff that best deepens our hearts. God intended that the dynamic of giving and receiving love from other people would enlarge our capacity to absorb His own pure love. Opening our hearts to other people helps us open our hearts to God. It's one more means of growing toward spiritual intimacy.

John, probably the disciple most intimately connected to Christ, highlights in his first Epistle the link between love and knowing God: "Everyone who loves has been born of God and knows God. Whoever does not love does not know God, because God is love" (1 John 4:7, 8). To the apostle the connection is infinitely clear: "Whoever loves his brother lives in the light" (1 John 2:10).

Usually this enlightening act of loving others doesn't involve some dramatic gesture. Often it has to do with our responses to everyday situations. All kinds of little choices determine whether or not we will live connectedly or disconnectedly. We have to push out the boundaries a little, stop when we want to walk by, reach out when we'd rather keep our hands in our pockets.

When the prophet Micah shouted, "Act justly," his call thudded against the insular world of Hebrew religion, safe inside its countless rituals.

"IT'S NONE OF MY BUSINESS"

Most men support each other from a respectful distance. If a guy's in trouble, we "let him handle it." Nobody wants to "butt in" and tell him how to run his life. This is OK in most situations. One thing that makes a man feel good is the ability to take care of business on his own.

But at times such an attitude turns into a liability. Sometimes support from a "respectful distance" isn't helpful at all. On occasion we need support that's up close and personal. A while back my friend Bill's wife went through a traumatic bout with obsessive-compulsive disorder. At the time I gave him only the usual sympathetic greetings. As a result, I had no idea that he was hanging on the end of his rope.

Sometime later I heard that the marriage of another friend was falling apart. Something about Derrick's face caught me as he broke the news. Those eyes that kept drifting to the sidewalk, the weariness in his voice—maybe it wasn't all that different from the expression of the homeless man.

That look pushed me across a line, forced me outside my usual boundary. We had to do something. I called up the other guys we played tennis with and said we should get together. Yeah, I know Derrick never talks much about stuff like that. Who does? But we can just play a few sets and see if he wants to open up afterward.

Well, as we sat on a bench toweling off and sucking in our middle-aged bellies after a hard-fought match, Derrick did want to talk. He wanted to a lot, as a matter of fact.

So we started getting together every Wednesday night. And after a couple weeks, the dam broke. Derrick explained that he realized how manipulative and controlling he'd been. He was trying hard to change. Mandy, however, couldn't trust him anymore. His voice was a grim monotone, but the jagged pain came through clearly. Bill talked a bit about the hellish low point in his own marriage and about how things had turned around.

When I glanced around, the guys were crying. And it was good. No one was embarrassed because everyone felt something of what Derrick felt. It was the first time in a long time that any of us had crossed that boundary, that "respectful distance," and it felt exhilarating. We were spilling our guts, showing concern, and praying for each other. Basic stuff. Calling out to the Lord to help a friend make it through.

Each week we had to precede our sessions, of course, with some in-your-face tennis and generous rounds of friendly insults. A few minutes after guaranteeing a guy across the net that I would personally smash the ball through his forehead I would then join the others in a circle and we'd begin praying our hearts out for him. All the yelling and screaming (in good humor) just loosened us up for the real fellowship afterward.

Continuing to share on Wednesday nights, we spilled even more out. We rallied around Jim who wanted to give the Five-Day Plan to Stop Smoking one last shot. And we encouraged Dan, whose wife was growing more and more distant, to hang in there.

What impressed me most about these encounters was how much happened just because we stepped a few feet over the line. It opened up a whole other world that had always been there, very close, but until then out of reach.

I found my heart unexpectedly deepened. God's love became intensely real to me because I was trying to give it away. In the struggle of seeking to help bring a little healing to broken human beings, the Wounded Healer Himself came very close to me.

Sometimes the best way to recapture intimacy with God is simply to give ourselves away. It's not that we'll always see Him act miraculously. The struggle itself is what counts. We come to feel a little of what God feels, are moved by what moves Him. His passion for servanthood, His endless stretching out, starts to get into our bones.

CROSSING THAT LINE

One Thursday evening I found myself at the homeless shelter again, and I decided to go beyond the usual routine of giving a polite greeting, handing the men their supper plates, showing them a video, and putting them down for the night. OK, maybe it wasn't so much my decision as the fact that the VCR wouldn't work. Anyway, there they were with nothing to do. So I asked myself, "How about stepping over the line?"

I noticed a few young Spanish guys finishing their spaghetti. Having grown up in Mexico and Colombia, I could communicate without any problem. Soon I learned that they were among those people who wait on street corners every morning, hoping for a truck to come by and give a few lucky ones eight hours of grueling labor for minimum wage. One guy in particular, Javier, warmed up to me, and I to him.

He proved to be a fascinating individual. Javier came from a good family in Mexico. His brother was a physician and had helped him get into a good university. But Javier had screwed up his chance. The usual detours of youth, I guessed. He kept mentioning *mis errores* (my errors) ruefully, and I realized how much loss lurked in those two words. Looking into his eyes and listening to his intelligent narrative, I felt the grief of one whose bright future was slipping out of reach.

Javier was trying to work his way up from the bottom. But it was a long journey. He felt the call to do the right thing, but then his buddies would talk him into going out drinking again.

That night we talked about God, too. "The path of perfection is so hard," Javier said. "Cutting off your eye if you lust after a woman. How can you be that pure?" What he'd seen of priests getting money out of impoverished congregations was enough to make one an atheist.

I began to share my faith, my picture of God. And as night gathered around us, it became much more than a Christian duty. Poking at the spaghetti stains on the paper tablecloth, I began spilling out some of my life too. How I'd wrestled with a debilitating habit. What I'd discovered about how God helps us grow.

Javier and I arranged to meet again. He loved to read, and I promised to give him one of my books.

It was heavy stuff, not the kind of conversation I expected in a homeless shelter. I'd crossed a boundary, and a whole world opened up, a whole new life.

Crossing boundaries doesn't just take us a few steps forward—it makes big things happen. God seems so eager to expand our modest gestures. Deciding to move beyond your routine prayers, for example, you get into a group and take serious aim at specific needs. Boom. Answers start to multiply. All of a sudden God seems hyperactive.

Or you decide to poke around the neighborhood to see if any unchurched people might be interested in studying the Bible. Boom. You never dreamed so many receptive individuals existed. It's as if they'd just been waiting for this.

That's the way it is. You cross a line, and God doesn't just give you a nice pat on the back—He makes something very special happen, something that touches eternity. When I look back and see how the Lord has responded to my meager gestures to cross a boundary, I can't help picturing a God who jumps up and down and waves His arms wildly. He's excited that He can show us a whole new world.

MAKING THE CONNECTION

I once asked a friend about the times he felt closest to God. Tim has a wonderful mind and is able to articulate brilliant insights about God's character and the plan of salvation. But he recalled that two simple acts had affected him most profoundly. Once in church he felt compelled by an appeal to place everything in his wallet in the offering plate. It turned out to be a considerable sum. But he had to give it all. On another occasion he dragged himself off to visit an acquaintance in real need even though it was extremely late and he wanted to go home.

Tim told me that at each of these times he'd experienced an intense sense of intimacy. It was after doing these things that he'd felt an overwhelming, mystical union with God. He said it was the closest he'd ever been to heaven.

We can't summon up such experiences at any time just by giving enough or visiting needy people enough. Nor can we "earn" intimacy through good works. Exquisite sensations of God's closeness don't happen that often. But stretching beyond ourselves does open us up to God. Moments do come when we have a chance to cross a boundary and establish a connection. And those moments can give us glimpses of the heavenly Father.

I see that connection in the ministry of an Albanian nun named Mother Teresa, who labored cheerfully in Calcutta among the poorest of the poor. Mother Teresa cared for the destitute and dying in a bottomless ocean of poverty. Today her sisters of the order Missionaries of Charity search the slums in their blue-and-white saris to pick up emaciated bodies lying in the streets and take them back to a shelter where the people can die with a measure of dignity, assured of God's love, surrounded by gentle hands and smiling human faces.

Mother Teresa's work does not operate by triage principles. It has no great economic impact or strategic value. She would describe it simply as "a beautiful work for God." But her ministry became one of the most powerful statements made in the twentieth century. She made connections in a world of disconnectedness, because she saw much more than disease-ridden, filthy bodies amid the refuse of Calcutta. In them she recognized Jesus in disguise, the one who said, "Whatever you did for one of the least of these brothers of Mine, you did for Me."

When this Albanian nun caressed some nameless face brought in off the streets and barely breathing, she felt she was touching Jesus. She once wrote this prayer for herself: "Dearest Lord, may I see You today and every day in the person of Your sick, and, whilst nursing them, minister unto You. Though You hide Yourself behind the unattractive disguise of the irritable, the exacting, the unreasonable, may I still recognize You, and say: 'Jesus, my patient, how sweet it is to serve You.'"

God is much closer, much more accessible, than many of us imagine. When we cross a boundary and open up our hearts to someone in need, we will suddenly find that it's God who is filling us. God's face comes close enough to bring us the feeling of intimacy.

Part Four

A Devotional Life
That Deepens Our Hearts

Chapter Nine

A Window in the Wall

One night my teenage son, Jason, and I brought our supper down to the family room to catch some TV. (He said he would allow me to watch the news during commercials on the "Unplugged" MTV show he insisted was a historic telecast.) After arranging our trays on the coffee table, I bowed my head to say grace silently, thinking, as usual, that I want to be a good example for my son, as opposed to bugging him about praying before every meal.

But just then someone called down from the kitchen, "Do you guys want some fruit punch?"

Immediately my head popped up and I answered, "Yeah, bring two glasses." Then I dug into the mashed potatoes.

Jason, however, had noticed more than I imagined and said dryly, "Wow, Dad! Some people are just so deep in prayer that they can't hear anything that goes on around them. Very impressive."

I had to laugh at his ironic dig, but it got me to thinking. When was the last time I was so deep in prayer that I tuned out everything else? In other words, when was the last time I really concentrated in prayer?

I've been praying for a long time now and should have this down pretty well. But I still find it easy for prayer to trickle off into thoughts about unpaid bills and the key football matchups this coming Sunday. It especially distresses me when I hear about mystics who spend hours in ecstatic contemplation.

Is it more difficult to concentrate these days, or is it just my imagination? We're constantly bombarded by fast-paced hype and images. Our world fairly pulsates with newer, brighter, quicker, slicker things—all designed to grab our attention.

But the thing that most dominates our lives is the incredible electronic "window" in the family room. You just press the remote and immediately zoom in on anything you want on cable. Wildebeests fording a river in the Serengeti. News analysts on the right and left pontificating past each other. Cops and home-boys shooting it out. People on talk shows sharing their most intimate secrets. Sitcoms, classic movies, every sport under heaven, game shows—it's all there. All you have to do is sit in front of the window. The stream of images entertain us without requiring any effort on our part.

By contrast, the task of closing our eyes and trying to carry on a conversation with the invisible God can be quite a challenge. Often it seems hard to handle anything more than a quick nod heavenward or a brief request about the things we want.

Let's face it—prayer gets boring. It's no problem to stay on your knees in an emergency. But the everyday stuff—that's another matter. Sometimes I feel like I'm praying at a wall—my tired phrases bounce back at me. I've said it all before.

In the back of my mind I know that this is a long, long way from intimacy. I'm a long way from admiring God.

All roads leading back to a sense of intimacy with God pass through the devotional life. There are no useful detours, no shortcuts. I've had to learn that fact again and again. If I'm serious about really grasping the height and breadth of Christ's love I have to get serious about the quality of my communication. What's happening to me when I pray? What's happening to me when I read the Bible? Am I building the kind of devotional life that will result in genuine intimacy?

In this section we'll explore ways to recover the bonding power of basic communication with God.

SEEING THROUGH THE WINDOW
Recently when I found myself praying at the wall again, I remembered

something that had once helped me greatly. And I began to realize that it was a kind of window, a window very different from the multi-channel window that mesmerizes so many of us now.

It appeared to me when I was working in Japan, commuting to and from an English language school every day. The vast metropolis of Osaka had started to get to me. Every day I would look across a station platform at all the expressionless commuter faces staring back through subway windows. Sometimes late at night on a bridge of the Yodo River another train would pass my 9:52 express going the other way. As I looked across at the figures in the yellow light—ghostlike faces disappearing into the dark—I would imagine lost souls in limbo.

A big city surrounds you with smirking ads, salacious posters, crowds of elbows, and countless staring eyes that never meet yours. The city can weigh down on you after a while. It's a gray desert of slick vices and squalid air.

Young and unmarried, I struggled with lust on an hourly basis. I'd been writing verses of Scripture in a little notebook and attempting to memorize them. At the time it seemed to me a matter of spiritual survival. I wanted God in my head somehow. But how was I supposed to communicate the power of Christ to my Japanese friends when acquiring a pure heart seemed about as easy to achieve as a moon landing?

One particular day, as I stared gloomily through the train window, the scene before my eyes switched as if I'd pressed a TV remote. It was a very ordinary afternoon. The train was rolling past a cluster of department stores—the same old, gray, impersonal wilderness.

But suddenly my investment in memorizing texts paid off. A line from Psalm 29 beamed into my head: "The voice of the Lord shakes the desert" (verse 8). *Boom.* I saw a little burst of light. Other verses rushed in. I recalled that the voice of the Lord is powerful, majestic, strikes with flashes of lightning, and makes us skip like a calf with joy.

Yes, it was good to have a God like that—in the heart of the city. His voice could accompany me. God's words, Psalm 12 said, "are flawless, like silver refined in a furnace of clay, purified seven times" (verse 6). Maybe it didn't matter so much if I was tired or depressed or lonely on the train. The words of the Lord were going off outside the window like fireworks.

Then I remembered that challenge Yahweh laid out before Pharaoh through Moses: "Let My people go that they may celebrate a feast to Me in the wilderness" (Ex. 5:1, NASB). The Lord didn't invite His people out to subsistence rations in the desert, didn't call them to exist on their survival skills. He summoned to a feast! And that's exactly what was happening to me. I was banqueting away on the Word right there in the urban desert with the same monotonous scenes passing before me, the same blank commuter faces all around. Looking out a different window, I could "taste and see that the Lord is good."

The little rush of Scripture left me exhilarated. It was the first time I had seen how powerfully God's Word could lift me out of my numbing environment.

CLEANING THE WINDOW WITH PRAISE

Now many years later I face a numbing environment of a different kind. The gray desert isn't just "out there"—it's in here, too. Secular indifference to the things of God gnaws at my bones. Other pursuits keep crowding out my prayers.

But I can try to find the window again. Maybe it's grown a bit grimy with time so that I can hardly see out of it. I don't have the fervor and imagination of youth. Perhaps it's even been boarded up.

Despite the obstacles, I want to look out of it again. I can't bear the thought of remaining a commuter the rest of my life and seeing only department stores pass by. I want to taste that feast in the wilderness again.

So I start cleaning the window.

First, I make my own personal collection of praise to prime the pump. Call it the "best of the Psalms." They are verses that make God vivid for me.

I enjoy the fact that El Shaddai can be overwhelmingly powerful:

"Our God is a consuming fire" (Heb. 12:29).

"The voice of the Lord shakes the desert" (Ps. 29:8).

"Mountains melt like wax before the Lord" (Ps. 97:5).

Yet this mighty outstretched arm of God has a gentle hand:

"A bruised reed he will not break.

and a smoldering wick he will not snuff out" (Isa. 42:3).

I love the picture in Psalm 65 of a God who both stills the tumult of the peoples and makes the dawn and sunset shout for joy (verses 7, 8). It suggests a

Being who combines in one personality profound peace and spectacular exuberance. I like people like that.

It's also intriguing to think about a God who is so intensely holy that "even the moon is not bright and the stars are not pure in his eyes" (Job 25:5), yet who is at the same time unfathomably solicitous toward sinners:

"Precious to me are your thoughts, O God!" (Ps. 139:17).

"By this I will know that God is for me" (Ps. 56:9).

I find the images of the Lord as our provider stimulating to ponder. This Good Shepherd, this Father to the fatherless, the One who visits the earth and causes it to overflow, who covers the meadows with flocks and the valleys with grain, can make me lie down in green pastures and will lead me beside still waters (Ps. 68:5, 6; 65:9, 13; 23:2). And He can do all that even in an urban wasteland.

That's how I start cleaning the window. I bounce my praises off something in Scripture that fires my imagination. If my prayers grow pedantic, I know that I've got a lot of help in the Bible—even if I'm not very mystical or naturally articulate. The Psalms give me 150 ways to compliment my heavenly Father. That's a pretty good start.

CLEANING THE WINDOW WITH PSALMS

The next thing I usually do is paraphrase a psalm. David and his colleagues had their own reasons for exulting in the Lord. Often David had just barely escaped another assassination attempt by King Saul. As he was catching his breath out in the Judean wilderness, he would express in a psalm heartfelt thanks for the rescue.

I have my own reasons for praise. God has rescued me in other ways—a check that comes through just in time, deliverance from overwhelming temptation, a conflict beautifully resolved. And so I apply the psalmist's expressions of praise to my own situations. I fit my own blessings into the verses and remember the highlights of my life, the times when I saw God clearly. I don't want to let go of those memories, and the best way to hold them is to seal them in a psalm.

CLEANING THE WINDOW WITH PRAYER

Finally, when I really need help in focusing my prayer, I select one divine character trait and think of all the reasons I appreciate it. Expanding on one of God's specific qualities tends to sharpen my praise. Considering His power, holiness, or mercy, for example, I recall all the biblical descriptions I can think of that relate to it, then I ponder God's acts in Scripture that exemplify it, and finally I remember acts of God I've witnessed that express it.

The point is to pick something specific that focuses my praise. Sometimes a theme helps. If it's raining, I'll think of all the ways God blesses through rain. If I've just said goodbye to an old friend who's been visiting, I'll praise God for all the beautiful people who've shown me what He's like. Or if the sky is cloudless when I wake up in the morning, I might praise Him for everything that is blue and good.

When I invest a little time in the discipline of praise, the wall really does dissolve and my prayers stop bouncing back at me. Praise creates a window in the wall, an opening that reveals wonderful scenes. It doesn't matter what method you use to look through the window, only that you make the effort. Praising isn't like falling off a chair. Human beings—even converted, believing human beings—don't just naturally erupt in continual praise to God.

It's a discipline. But after all, I put effort into all kinds of communication. I can work for weeks on end to find the right story for a script or might go over some little talk with the boss countless times in my head. But how much do I invest in the quality of my communication with God?

Of course, prayer is supposed to come spontaneously from the heart. God doesn't want to hear pious rehearsed speeches. But if I'm just mumbling the same old lines, then I need something to wake me up. To put some color back in my limp prayers, I need to focus the mind. A huge difference exists between a halfhearted thought aimed heavenward and a message I *will* to God, something I really mean.

Our natural tendency in prayer is to touch every base except that of God Himself. We tug at His blessings, intercede for others, or express thanks for the trees, our job, new furniture, and sunny days. We do everything but focus on the person of God. Private praise is the best way we have of looking directly at Him, of talking directly to Him.

It's essential for intimacy. Closeness is about being face-to-face and eye-to-eye. Couples who are having problems can rarely hold each other's gaze for long. They tend to look away when talking about personal things. But people who are trying to get close pick up on each other's every facial expression. We treasure the face that we stare at and enjoy the qualities of the loved one that we describe. Affection spoken out loud leaves a deeper impression.

That's why the discipline of praise can deepen our hearts. It's a way of talking directly to God about the way we feel toward Him and of getting our affection out in the open. The best praise is not just a recitation of the right theology, but an expression of admiration. Instead of just listing what He's done for us lately, we focus on Him—period.

SEEING GOD IN EVERYTHING

My two brothers and I were mountain biking in the hills above Santa Barbara one afternoon when I had to wimp out. They wanted to conquer a ridge about half a mile ahead. I'd been battling flu and didn't feel up to the last stretch, so I told them I'd wait where I was.

It was a beautiful day. The sky above me rolled clear blue all the way down to the ocean. The air was dry and sweet. Sitting beside a scrawny cactus, I watched my brothers growing smaller and smaller on the bluff.

For some reason I felt it was great just to wait. It was good to have absolutely nothing to do. The silence and stillness of the rocky landscape began to sink in. I wanted to be still too. And I began to praise.

God really did stretch from horizon to horizon. He encompassed the entire scene. I could sense His bigheartedness, because all of creation seemed indescribably good. The little, unassuming plants beside me were performing miracles in the arid soil. Each one had its own intricate beauty. The ridges high above me made dramatic lines against the sky. I could almost see the curve of the earth in the broad stretch of ocean below.

In those moments before my brothers returned I sensed a stretching and pulling in my own heart. Having stepped out of myself, I managed a bit of genuine adoration. I felt how powerful that direct line to God can be. Only God mattered there in that delicious quiet. And He was more than sufficient.

SEEING GOD IN NOTHING

Strangely enough, I discovered the same thing through an experience exactly the opposite. Instead of sitting up on a mountaintop, I was down in the pits, lying on my bed late one night, wondering how to break off an obsessive, destructive relationship. I knew I had to do it—the emotions were killing me. But it seemed saying goodbye was going to destroy me too.

Everything had become so intense and conflicted inside me that I seemed to be suffocating. There was no air. No blue sky. No eloquent creation. Just a messed-up me, alone with my impossible task. After wrestling with God and with Scripture, I finally saw a way to end the relationship decisively so the problem wouldn't trip me up again. I gave myself up to the task, telling the Lord, "You set up the time and place, and I'll be there."

Everything still felt dark and impossible, but I began to praise. I tried to say yes with my heart as well as my head. And the more I praised, the more certain I became. A window opened up a very different view. Yes, I wanted to put my whole miserable self in His hands. Yes, He had guided me expertly in the past. Yes, we've had such wonderful times together.

As I continued talking directly to God about my feelings, the great immovable object bearing me down became light. I wasn't suffocating anymore. It was good to give this up for such a wonderful Christ, good to endure this pain in order to be faithful to Him. Any sacrifice was a privilege. Yes, it was every bit as good as the stillness on a mountain in the middle of a gorgeous day.

I don't know that I have ever felt such love for the Lord. That dark night I had been widened a bit—yes, pushed and pulled again until room opened in my heart, some good room for intimacy.

Chapter Ten

With the Eyes
of an Artist

E scaping the glare of a blazing southern California sky, I walked into Loma
Linda University Library and disappeared in its innermost bowels—the
stacks. That's where it stores the bulk of the books—and where people who
spend their lives doing serious research hang out. The musty smell of yellowing
pages and old print surrounded me, as did a slight feeling of claustrophobia.

But I'd come in search of Jesus—and found Him. A volume on the third
floor had sketches by Rembrandt. Another art book on the fourth floor contained several portraits by nineteenth-century painters. In still another I found a
dramatic Crucifixion scene by Rubens.

Settling into a little study cubicle unclaimed by any of the resident
researchers, I set up my camera and lights as quietly as possible. I was working
on a film in which students from a variety of countries and religious back-
grounds talked about how they had encountered Christ. It was sort of a United
Nations portrait of the Saviour, and I needed something visual that would tie all
the stories together. The art books gave me my answer. I could cut in the best
work of artists who tried to depict the most fascinating Person in history.

To simulate a little motion with the portraits, I experimented at length with
panning and zooming and moving the artwork around. Before I knew it, the
morning had passed in the dim stacks. After a quick sandwich it was back to
peering through the camera again. So many great paintings. I found myself run-

ning up and down the stairs, retrieving and returning the dusty tomes that cradled masterpieces. It almost felt like grand theft as I cleaned out the place, stealing all those incredible images and storing them on film cartridges I kept stuffing in my pockets. How was I going to get permission to use all this stuff? I'd think about that later.

Finally I finished. I'd spent nine hours hovering over those books, but I had every image worth having—the best and the brightest. And then I remembered the prayer. It was only after stowing my gear and slipping the last book back into its appointed place that it hit me.

That morning I had made a special petition. Tired of trudging through one workday after another without ever giving God a second thought, I wanted that day to be different. Although I greeted Him in the morning like a dutiful Christian, after that we never seemed to have occasion to speak. I always just slid into my busy routine.

So I had resolved on that day to try to keep in touch, to say hello once in a while. I wanted some evidence that I wasn't just a secular person with a bit of religion around the edges. In short, I wanted to see Jesus in the swirl of everyday events.

As I descended the narrow stairway in the stacks, I realized I'd been staring at Him intently for nine hours. Poring over that noble brow, that determined chin, those compassionate eyes, I'd been looking at Him until my eyes blurred from the strain. And yet I'd never once given the Man Himself a thought. The day had gone by, and our paths had not crossed in any tangible way. I had scores of Christs in my pockets, but absolutely nothing in my head or heart.

SEEING WITH THE EYES OF A NEW BELIEVER

The film has been finished for some time, the portraits of Christ edited into the flow of testimony. But it remains for me an incomplete project, because now I sense more than ever the challenge of getting what's on the page to register somehow. I still want to see Jesus, and I still keep missing Him.

Take the Gospels, for example. I've been listening to those stories since I was in kindergarten. Yes, I know about the woman at the well and the water of life, the stilling of the storm, and the cleansing of the lepers. It's all so familiar that it hardly registers. I stare at the images, I study my Bible like a good Christian, but the words seem to have lost their power. The "good news" seems to have turned into the "same old story."

When we are new in the faith, doesn't it seem as if God is speaking His Word audibly? It's all so fresh and exciting. He's telling us things we never realized before, opening up a new world. It's an age of discovery.

But after we "mature" in the faith, we often lose that sense of a still-speaking Word. God's message just lies there on the page—having been verbalized in another time, another place. We work hard to see the context, to reconstruct layers of meaning. While we may even know the nuances of the Greek, it's a religious text, not a revealing voice that speaks directly to each of us.

This seems to happen a lot to people who grow up in the church. They can't figure out what all the new converts are jumping up and down about. Wide-eyed new believers run up to them, excitedly pointing out some "fantastic promise" that's been around 2,000 years, or speaking ecstatically about "discovering something wonderful" that's perfectly obvious in the Gospel narrative.

The Bible appears different in the hands of new believers. It's as if it has electricity running through its pages; it makes things happen. And so some of us who've been around a while keep looking back and forth from the crumpled, heavily underlined Bibles of new Christians to our own. Comparing the two, we say to ourselves, "Hey, mine must not be working. How do you plug this thing in?"

I want the Bible to be a voice that still speaks. I want it to flow with some electricity. In trying to find a way to see Jesus again (while I'm looking straight at Him) I've sought to isolate what it is exactly that turns on the Bible for people. We may not be able to recapture the bubbly emotional momentum of new converts, but perhaps we can learn to look through their eyes. How do they see what we don't? As I think about this I remember when the Word became electric for me.

A WORD WITHOUT MEANING

When I was growing up, the Bible was a little like the original Model T. You could have it in any color you wanted as long as it was black. The only Word of God we knew came in solemn black leather and inscrutable King James English.

It wasn't a book people cozied up to or enjoyed reading. Most of my elders carried it around in order to make a statement. And those who studied it most diligently seemed most devoted to winning arguments with it.

At a certain age I concluded that real men and women read the Bible all the way through—straight through. If the Bible is medicine for the soul, then people ought not take just a spoonful, but should chugalug the whole bottle.

So I started in on Genesis. The stories of the patriarchs weren't too bad. Abraham, Isaac, and Jacob helped me pick up a little steam. And there was enough action in the wilderness wanderings to keep me going. But then I ran into the real test of manhood or womanhood: Leviticus. I learned about burnt offerings, grain offerings, guilt offerings, sin offerings, fellowship offerings—I thought they would never end. When I'd finally slogged through all that, I ran into five chapters on what the priests wore. Along about the tenth description of a ram's entrails, I finally gave up and turned back to Egypt—along with the rest of those spineless Israelites.

Somehow I just couldn't get through Leviticus although I tried four or five times. I'd go back to Genesis, get a good running start, and *bam!* Leviticus would get me every time. My spiritual manhood was still in question.

But then one day in church I found a little blue card that listed various Bible books and chapter numbers. It was the Junior Bible Reading Plan. By marking off a chapter a day, a person could get through the whole Bible in one year. Most important, it outlined a condensed version of Scripture. The reading plan skipped some chapters—you didn't have to read the gross parts, I guess. And they left out my nemesis Leviticus altogether. I could do this.

Faithfully I read every morning, trying to do the right thing, and I did get through the Bible. But usually, after I'd finished a chapter and marked my little blue card, I couldn't remember a thing I'd read. It was just a blur.

During most of my youth the Bible remained a familiar stranger. I knew all the stories, and yet it was a foreign book. God wasn't speaking my language, wasn't touching my world. The Word of God was like a boring houseguest who won't stop talking. Someone you wish you hadn't invited for supper.

I reverenced God's Word. My mother told me two things that stuck with me like statutes from Sinai: place coat hangers in the closet with the hook facing in, and don't put anything on top of the Bible.

I honored the Word—but mine wasn't plugged in. And I had little idea that these words could shine like neon signs—until my sophomore year in college.

MAKING IT REAL

At Western Illinois University I became acquainted with some students who were active in Campus Crusade for Christ, and they invited me to a weekend Bible camp. Now, many forces at work inside me wanted to say no to the invitation. The stuffy, black leather King James culture; the ill-fitting, starchy cloak of religion; and the verbosity of the Bible all turned me off.

But the angels had someone on their side. Her name was Michelle—long dark hair, brilliant blue eyes, painfully cute. She was one of the Campus Crusade people. I'd run into her a few times in between classes and had fallen headlong into that state of infatuation where you see light and truth wherever the person you adore goes. If Michelle had suddenly transferred to the University of Albania, then I'm sure Albania would have appeared to offer the greatest educational experience on earth.

Michelle was going to this camp. And her face sort of obliterated those of all the stuffed shirts I had known.

I went. And God in His mercy managed to reach through the thick haze I was in and teach me something wonderful. One of the leaders at the camp introduced a method of Bible study I'd never heard of before. It consisted simply of observation, interpretation, and application.

This is how it works. You look carefully at a passage, noticing all the details. Then you interpret what the events or sayings in the passage mean. Next you try to apply a principle from the passage to your own life. How can I use this? What do I need to do to make it real?

Fortunately, the people at the retreat didn't just give us the theory—they helped us put it into practice. Each morning after the first session, everyone had what they called "quiet time." I remember us filtering out into the forest. It was an Illinois fall, and the leaves were just starting to turn. Everyone found their spot under a tree and opened the Word of God.

I'll never forget that scene. It was so different from the religion of toeing the line and putting square pegs in square holes. Instead of focusing on getting all the doctrines right, it was about meeting God. Suddenly I had stepped out of a closet into an enormous, richly decorated room. As I looked into the Bible carefully and prayerfully, I was amazed at all that I could see right under my nose.

That weekend divided my relationship with the Word into night and day. Before, I had never made personal discoveries in the Bible. Afterward, they came by the handful.

LOOK UNTIL YOU CAN ADMIRE

I've thought a lot about what made the difference and don't think it was just this particular method of Bible study. Observation, interpretation, and application aren't magical in themselves. Many other tools have also helped people plug into the Word.

The best way I can explain it is to say that I learned to be an artist.

Think of the way painters observe nature. They're looking at the same trees, mountains, and seascapes that everyone else sees and have seen it all before, just like we have. A tree's a tree. Yet somehow they keep finding inspiration. In fact, they find themselves driven to keep painting year after year, often enduring poverty and isolation.

Why did Claude Monet keep doing canvases of the same old water lilies? Why did Van Gogh find himself drawn again and again to those same wheat fields in southern France? And how do they make people see the world differently as a result?

If we could condense their secret into one phrase, I think it would be: look until you can admire. Artists don't observe to memorize or to quantify or even to master—they look to admire. They find something extraordinary in the ordinary. Nature speaks to them.

We glance at a line of trees and read "generic green," while artists spot 25 different shades of the color.

Or we see a bunch of faces in the street that we lump into the category "generic strangers," while they detect lines of sorrow, shades of anxiety, flickers of joy.

I think that's what we were doing under our trees in that Illinois autumn.

We were looking until we could admire. When I could get my mind off trying to find which tree Michele was under, I did search for the 25 shades of green in God's Word. I read until the generic faces broke into distinct expressions.

That's what I need to recover today. To seek intimacy with God is to take the time to admire Him in His Word, to look until I can see something new to admire. The reason so many of us stop hearing the voice in the Word is that it has become for us a catechism. Considering it a collection of correct information, we go to it to review what we think we have already learned. We're just getting the facts down a little more pat.

If the Bible is just a textbook, we'll never plug ourselves into it. I know. I do a lot of research for my writing, and I can come away from an hour of study with no more inspiration than if I'd been underlining a volume on chemistry.

Catechisms are nice, but they just don't deepen our hearts. Only a certain kind of looking can do that. It's only when we see the face behind all the words, or the Person behind all the portraits, that God can stretch us.

Sometimes when we know everything, we forget that the point is not to know everything, but to admire, to make personal discoveries. That's why God wants to give us the "Spirit of wisdom and revelation." It's so that "the eyes of your heart may be enlightened" (Eph. 1:17, 18).

After nine hours of poring over masterpieces in the library stacks, I still couldn't see with the eyes of my heart. I need to remember what it was like sitting under the Illinois tree and viewing with the eyes of an artist.

A FRESH LOOK AT A FAMILIAR STORY

Consider the story of the paralytic at the Pool of Bethesda. I once thought I knew all there is to know about it. But one day I tried to see more.

The paralytic lay waiting, watching the sun crawl across the blank sky overhead. Several other residents of Bethesda had also dragged themselves close to the water, imagining that a breeze strong enough to stir the pungent odors of the nearby Sheep Gate market might help the angel who sometimes disturbed the pool. Others waited nearby, having trained themselves to detect a faint rumbling underground that usually preceded the bubbling of water to the surface.

They were all waiting for the miracle, each believing—or trying to believe—that the occasional bubbling of water was an angel come down from heaven. First one in gets healed.

Jerusalem was in the midst of a great holy feast, and Jesus had come as a good Jew to participate in the elaborate rituals of the Temple. But on this high Sabbath day He'd left the pomp and pageantry behind for some fresh air and been drawn to His more natural environment—the dark corners where the poor and afflicted huddled.

Jesus walked through the covered colonnades surrounding a spring-fed pool called Bethesda. He looked out over the human wreckage hovering about it. Pale bodies racked by disease panted on filthy mats, their faces turned toward the motionless surface. The blind crouched on the stone porches, their heads cocked, ready to spring toward the first sound of water lapping on stone. The maimed sprawled in a variety of positions, trying to keep their good limbs ready for propulsion. And the most pathetic, those completely paralyzed, lay near the water, staring up at the cold columns, hoping against hope.

Glancing around at those gray faces dying of suspense, Jesus longed to cause a real disturbance by healing them all. But He knew that such a mighty work during a feast day in a Jerusalem bulging with pilgrims would cut short His ministry. Overenthusiastic crowds had already prevented Him from ministering in certain areas.

So He zeroed in on one particularly hopeless case—a man who'd been an invalid for 38 years. Walking over to him, Jesus asked a simple question: "Do you want to get well?"

Looking with the eyes of an artist who tries to notice everything, I first wondered why He asked that. On the surface it seems like a stupid question. Of course, the man wanted to get well. Why else would he expose himself to cold and heat every day amid those stinking colonnades?

But when I pondered that simple question a bit more, something clicked, and I saw something to admire. Jesus was presenting Himself as a servant. He wasn't parading through the area as a great miracle worker who condescended to pass His wand over some lucky wretch. Our Lord asked if He might be of help. What a nice touch. His power, always tempered by grace, was never overbearing. The One who stilled storms as if quieting a naughty child, the One who multiplied bread for multitudes and made demons flee, the One whom even corpses obeyed—He's the one who asked politely, "Do you want to get well?" It's an irrepressible servant's "May I help you?"

And yes, it was also His way of dropping a little hope into the well of despair. It was like the first morsel a starving person gets to prepare for the feast to come.

The paralytic, of course, could think only of the pool. He'd managed to persuade acquaintances to carry him to Bethesda, but no one wanted to hang around all day waiting for the water to move. Maybe, just maybe, this kind Stranger would give him a push at the right time.

Seizing this ray of hope, Jesus bent it from superstition to Himself. He looked into the man's eyes and uttered a perfectly ridiculous command: "Get up! Pick up your mat and walk." He might as well have told the stone columns to dance in a circle around the afflicted.

But those muted nerve endings and shriveled limbs did respond, and the invalid struggled to his feet. Thirty-eight years of immobility faded away like a head cold. Nice touch indeed.

"Do you want to get well?" I'd never seen such a startling glimpse of Jesus the servant. He was finally coming off the page and deepening my heart.

Look until you can admire. Look with the eyes of an artist.

Chapter Eleven

Admire Until You Can Express

The stocky guard with bushy eyebrows glanced through a barred window in a prison near Havana. He could hardly believe his eyes as a small black book crawled along the corridor in front of Cell 107. Quickly unlocking the heavy door that separated him from the cell block, he walked in. The book had stopped moving. But bending down, he noticed that it was attached to a long thread that extended down both directions of the corridor. He followed one end of the thread and came to the cell of a particularly troublesome prisoner, Humberto Noble Alexander.

"What's going on here?" the guard demanded. Without waiting for an answer, he yanked the book to him and picked it up. Glancing through the pages, the semiliterate son of the revolution got an idea that it was a religious book. He glared at Humberto. "You know you're not supposed to have Christian propaganda in here!"

Humberto approached the bars and replied, "Oh, but I have special permission to have this book."

"What do you mean 'special permission'?"

"It's right there inside the book."

The guard looked inside the front and back covers. "There's nothing in here."

The prisoner reached his hand out. "Let me see the book, and I'll show you."

The guard thought a moment, then handed the suspicious volume through the bars.

Trying not to betray his relief at having the book in his hands, Humberto turned to Acts 5:29 and read: " 'We must obey God rather than men!' " "You see," he said, smiling, "I have permission—it's written right here."

The guard's eyebrows began to quiver as he suspected that he'd been had, and he demanded, "Give me back that thing!"

Humberto stepped back from the bars with the book in both hands. "I can't do that."

The guard began yelling, but Humberto wouldn't give up his prize.

A prison regulation prohibited any guard from opening a prisoner's cell without another officer present. So the man had to run to get his commandant. When he returned, the book was nowhere in sight. Humberto was lying on his bunk as if nothing had happened, but he had a pleased expression on his face.

When the commandant found out exactly how the forbidden Bible had been lost, he divided his time between excoriating the guard for his stupidity and threatening to punish Humberto if he didn't reveal where the book had gone.

They never found the Bible, even though they tore apart Humberto's cell. But they made the stubborn prisoner pay dearly with a vicious flogging.

Humberto had endured worse. He'd done time in "the box of death," in which the guards crammed 10 men together to suffocate or lose their sanity. Already they had shot and starved and electrocuted him. During 20 years of confinement in one of Castro's worst prisons he had learned to endure much. But the one thing he could not endure was to be without the Word of God.

And so a few days later Humberto retrieved that small black Book from a drainage pipe connected to his cell, dangling from a long gray thread, and began passing it back and forth from cell to cell once more. Each man in that cell block had his allotted time with the Bible that Humberto had taught them all to cherish.

EXPRESSING THROUGH ACTIONS

Humberto Noble Alexander—the same man who had in Israel played David to my friend Darryl's Goliath—is the most extraordinary man I have ever met. The first time I saw him was the day I interviewed him in preparation for a television program. At the time I just couldn't put this bright-eyed, cheery face together with the horror stories he was telling. He had nothing of the martyr about him. When I drove him to East Los Angeles to see old prison comrades, it struck me how much these otherwise profane men revered him as their spiritual leader.

I don't think I really understood what the Bible can mean to a person until I met Humberto. It wasn't just the tremendous sacrifices he had made to preserve his copy of the Scriptures, but the joy he took in its words, the sense of an immediate connection with Christ. He assured me repeatedly that this Word was what had sustained him through his long imprisonment.

The image that stays with me is that of the little black Book crawling along the prison corridor. Humberto's Bible was always in motion, always sharing its life-giving message with other prisoners. His Bible was always doing something. He wielded it as a powerful weapon when everything around him conspired to keep him powerless.

Humberto taught me something I have ever since tried to remember. It's quite simple. The Bible comes alive when we use it. After we look until we can admire, we need to admire until we find something to express.

The Bible becomes electric in our hands when we experiment with it, express it through actions. It is not just about finding more rules to follow or getting doctrines right. Rather it's about wanting to declare something great about God through our lives. That's the kind of devotional life that will deepen our hearts.

Instead of just putting in time with the Word, I need to make my own discoveries and find something I want to express through my life.

The Word is a living thing, a seed that—when planted—can spring into life. If we give it half a chance, it will expand our lives immeasurably. When Paul urges us to let the Word of Christ dwell in us richly, he describes people teaching and admonishing, singing psalms and spiritual songs with gratitude in their hearts to God (Col. 3:16). The Word needs to be expressed.

EXPANDING OUR WORLDS

I was in my Osaka apartment early one morning reading the Bible and trying to see with the eyes of an artist, when some texts began to dig into me. They were familiar exhortations: "Build up one another." "Encourage one another." But as I stared out the window at our bonsai tree, I felt moved to pray for something to happen. I was tired of the usual petition: "Help me to be a good teacher and a good friend today." Now I felt an urge to rip these verses from the page, take them out into the next 16 waking hours, and make them do something. Surely, somewhere I could have a specific rendezvous with God's will.

So I said, "Lord, lead me to someone I can really help today." That prayer was not your everyday nod toward goodness—I wanted to be aimed at a target.

I went through my English classes as usual, then we had our normal staff meeting. No Japanese students threw themselves at my ankles and begged me to show them the light. But after the staff meeting a teacher named Peggy stopped me in the hallway. "I need to talk to you," she said with an unsettling directness. "Can we go somewhere?"

We walked to an empty classroom, and there she spilled her innermost feelings. Peggy felt like a fake, didn't know why she'd ever come to Japan. She unleashed a flood of insecurity and inadequacy. Hints of an extremely dysfunctional family background came through her words. As Peggy talked, the English teacher dissolved into a hurting, fearful child.

The rest of us had pigeonholed her as a loudmouth. Not the easiest to like. Now I saw deeper.

Nothing like this had ever happened to me before. I had not been much of a listener or a shoulder to cry on. Just the old male cliché: quiet, self-sufficient, content with work and an occasional game of football. My roommate and I exchanged maybe five sentences during my senior year in college. And we were good friends.

But on that occasion I was God's rendezvous. And so I became all ears, trying to understand her vulnerability. Somehow I managed to offer a few suggestions on how to acquire a stable spiritual life.

The Word did something that day. It pushed me beyond the typical male limitations and expanded my world.

And God seemed extremely close. We were in sync. I wasn't just out there winging it, trying to do my Christian duty as God looked down approvingly from

His omniscient vantage point. No, I was in motion with Him. We'd made contact at a point of need, and that interaction proved exhilarating.

Admittedly, rendezvous like that don't happen every day. But I believe they can happen much more frequently than we suspect. The Word can propel us to a specific point more often than we realize. We just need to admire until we have something to express.

I've found certain kinds of Bible study naturally seem to lend themselves to this process. In order to get something to express, it helps if we start at the center.

FOCUS ON THE CENTER

Christ is the center of everything when we study Scripture with the eyes of an artist. He is the Word perfected, at full strength, flawless and fully expressed. So begin (and end) by looking at Him as intently as possible. Notice every gesture. Try to hear the inflection in His words. Spotlight the economy and surgical precision of His every action. Watch for the reactions of those around Him. Check out every participant in His encounters—publicans, Pharisees, lepers, scribes, beggars, fallen women, disciples, multitudes, lawyers, corpses, His mother, rulers. Try to climb into the scenes: feel the weather, touch the faces, sense expectation, danger, and suspense. Imagine Christ's emotions. And *always* relate your impressions to the whole Person you are attempting to know.

Seeing as an artist means we become participants as much as possible. Instead of just standing on the sidelines snapping random photographs, we try to capture the shades of color, the textures, the mood, the barely visible harmonies and rhythms. We seek to feel as well as understand. Putting ourselves into the scenes helps bring it all home. Taking in the counsel, hope, conviction, encouragement, reprimands, and love, we incorporate them into our own lives. Such in-depth looking motivates us to flesh out those insights through our lives.

FOCUS ON CHARACTERS

From this key figure, we move to supporting members of the cast of Scripture. Biographical studies often yield new pictures out of familiar historical narratives. Try fashioning whole portraits from what we know of the lives of

Joshua, Solomon, and Nebuchadnezzar. What character traits do they exhibit? How did God woo, correct, and reward them? Putting together the pieces of a life can help us to see more intently. We can view Christ reflected in a variety of ways through such human characters: Moses pleading for wayward Israel, Jonathan befriending his rival, Daniel standing firm in an alien nation—they all add their colors to the primary picture.

FOCUS ON THEMES

Some biblical characters—the prophets—have made statements with their lives, producing bodies of work that document their religious passion, usually concentrated on the two essentials of judgment and redemption. The prophets speak with great conviction, but their messages can blur together. We can get lost in long passages against Moab and Edom or in oracles outlining a hoped-for kingdom that we have never seen. Thematic studies can help us see here. Each prophet does have a unique voice, and his passion does have its own shape. Try to uncover what he's emphasizing, what is unique about him. Draw a dominant message out of his "Thus saith the Lord."

Jeremiah's uncompromising call for proud, corrupt Jerusalem to surrender gives structure to almost all his messages. It echoes down to those of us who cling stubbornly to a threatened ego. Daniel had a habit of always focusing on God's sovereignty at the end of long passages full of symbolic beasts. That's a particularly meaningful point for a man who'd been waiting 70 years for God to restore His people.

Finding such themes can help us admire the whole when the details don't seem particularly inspiring. It reminds us that there's a point to it all. The prophets delivered fiery warnings and offered glorious hope in an attempt to move their people toward a certain kingdom, a certain point in time when the Christ would fulfill both judgment and redemption through His crucifixion and resurrection.

FOCUS ON PARAPHRASE

Themes help us get a handle on the prophets, but when it comes to the Epistles, the themes seem to spill over each other. Truths and principles crowd each other in Paul's run-on sentences. Peter and John are no theological lightweights either.

Taking each verse apart is one way to add up the meaning, but another method is more directly devotional. Try doing a verse-by-verse paraphrase of a passage. The Epistles contain many words and phrases that time has worn down to clichés. "Cleansed by the blood," "walking in the light," "victory in Christ," "justified," "sanctified"—such labels soon become invisible because they are so familiar. They serve as a kind of shorthand for great theological truth, but when we see and hear them again and again, the wealth of original meaning shrinks in our minds. We know but don't feel.

Paraphrasing can help us rediscover something to express. Rewriting the Word is a practice similar to what artists do when they sketch a scene. They begin to see what's out there by trying to capture it on canvas. A good definition of what paraphrasing does is found in Edward Hopper's explanation of his work: "My aim in painting has always been the most exact transcription possible of my most intimate impressions of nature." Paraphrasing helps to give voice to our innermost impressions of the Word. Writing them out is one way of reflecting the Bible's meaning back to God and letting it sink even deeper into us.

Read a sentence carefully, try to catch the significance of each word, dig for something concrete behind the abstractions, then write down what the sentence means in your own words. It's a way of expressing the faith of Scripture in a personal way. If Paul advises in Romans 12:21 "Do not be overcome by evil, but overcome evil with good," you might translate: "Don't let Satan push you around; you push Satan around—with Christ." When you read in 2 Peter 1:4 that God "has given us his very great and precious promises, so that through them you may participate in the divine nature," you might respond: "Just think, these incredible promises in the Bible are a means to share in the character qualities of God Himself!" Our sketches of Scripture will help us to see more actively and can lead us back to that essential goal: feeling deeper admiration, finding something to express.

Writing his brother Theo about inspiration, Vincent van Gogh spoke gratefully about times when "the sincerity of one's feeling for nature" becomes so strong that "one works without knowing one works . . . the strokes come with a sequence and a coherence like words in a speech or a letter." This is both art and the devotional life at its best. The Spirit wants to create in us a strong response to the Word that moves us to work without knowing we work, expressing in our lives something wonderful about the God we admire.

Look until you can admire.

Admire until you find something to express.

That's how the Word can come alive in our hands, how it can deepen our hearts so we can experience a very present God. The Word set in motion is the Word that brings Him close.

EXPRESSING TO EACH OTHER

I saw this most clearly during one of those Wednesday night meetings with the guys. Derrick was having trouble in his marriage, and the previous week we had each agreed to find a verse of Scripture that might encourage him. We middle-aged men were no Bible scholars. One or two had only a passing acquaintance with the Word. But we had a job to do. And so everyone stumbled around in the Scriptures until they found something useful.

That night, after our heated sets of tennis, we stood out in the parking lot under amber streetlights. Each of us dug out a piece of paper on which we'd written a verse for Derrick. Some had a hard time reading their scrawled writing in the dim light. But there was something special about our voices out there in the chill of the evening. The Word really was spoken—it was expressed. Going around the circle one by one, we talked about what we hoped these words could mean. We passed along our slips of paper, then prayed our blessing on him. Although we may have felt a bit awkward and self-conscious, we were holding Derrick up to God so the Word could become real to him.

The Word doesn't take you close to God because you analyze it expertly, or even because you study it diligently. Intimacy requires something more. The Word comes alive when you pass it on ragged slips to each other in the dark. With each movement it becomes something precious that binds you together— almost like the Bible passed on a thread down a prison corridor.

Part Five

Misfortunes
That Deepen Our Hearts

Chapter Twelve

The Symptom
Is the Cure

I thought I was going to get an answer when the nurse drew my dark blood into her clear vial under the fluorescent clinic lights. The walls were white, the nurse wore white. Clean, white paper stretched over the examining table. Everything looked antiseptically precise. I ought to be able to get my problem written down in black and white.

Well, the tests did decipher my blood. They did find the Epstein-Barr virus and were even able to identify its three different stages and determine how much I had of each variety.

But the doctor who gave me the results also told me the truth: "We don't really know that Epstein-Barr is the cause of chronic fatigue syndrome. It could well be that a large segment of the population has this virus in their blood, but only some come down with CFS symptoms."

I thanked him for his honesty, paid the bill, and went back to square one. Still no clear cause existed for CFS—and still no effective treatment.

By a process of elimination, a few physically maladjusted souls in the world reluctantly conclude that they have chronic fatigue syndrome. It's a little like being chosen last for a pickup basketball game. "Hey, you without any respectable curable disease to claim, you get CFS."

Diagnosing CFS is another way of saying, "We can't figure out why you're sick all the time, yet we don't want to say you're making it all up." Basically, the disease makes you feel as though you're coming down with the flu—permanently.

I do my downtime, spending one or two weeks in bed every few months. It's manageable most of the year. But sometimes I have bad spells that make me wonder if I'll be an invalid the rest of my life. The worst part is that I feel as though I have no rational reason for being flat on my back. Although the bed rest does not seem to be helping, if I try to get up and work I get worse. So for the most part I submit to this ambiguous state. Then every few days I crawl out of bed to see if I can remain on my feet without collapsing again.

Living in limbo is hard. A pretty driven person, I work independently on a contract basis for various clients because I'm more productive that way. Sitting down at the computer, I churn it out. So downtime comes as a personal affront.

I'm rather physical, too. For me, tennis, football, and basketball are not accessories, bits of recreation to keep me in shape for my real life. They're part of what life is all about. Blood pumping, muscles thumping, pushing myself to exhaustion—that's when I feel most alive.

So I don't take kindly to lying there between the sheets, waiting out another spell of CFS. It makes me feel as if I'm 90. But I'm not ready for a nursing home and don't want a trip to the bathroom to become my adventure for the day.

Since I'm loath to see myself as a 43-year-old invalid, I've dealt with CFS by obsessively seeking a cure. I figure one's got to exist somewhere, and if I try enough things, I'm sure to hit on something that works.

So here's my list, in rough chronological order.

1. Deep rest. If I sleep hard long enough instead of thrashing around in bed, my rest quotient will eventually reach critical mass and overwhelm chronic fatigue.

Dream on.

2. Ignore it. I'm not really sick, so I'll just keep working. Don't push it too hard, but stay on my feet.

Eventually I crash.

3. Barley green. High-potency nutrients will zap my lame immune system into working order.

Still waiting.

4. Cut sugar out of my diet, as well as anything else that might taste good.

No observable long-term effect except vivid dreams of apple pie à la mode.

5. Heavy-duty enemas?

Hey, I may be desperate, but I have standards.

6. New Age medicine?

Yeah, right. Maybe in another life.

7. Megadoses of vitamins B_{12} and C. Somebody once told me this regimen cured them. (I've concluded that people get "cured" by whatever they're trying at the time the disease finally gives up, but it's worth a try.)

It only gives me expensive urine.

8. Engage in moderate exercise instead of giving in to the fatigue.

Now I really crash.

9. Regular doses of zinc and iron.

I'm starting to develop a taste for heavy metal music, but . . . still waiting.

10. OK, cut out all sugar and saturated fats and give up sports for a year. See if it makes a difference long-term.

Giving up all that almost seems worse than CFS.

WAITING FOR THE "MAGIC BULLET"

I try all these things because I don't want to be a victim. It's frightening to think that I'm not in control of my own body. And CFS can seem to have a mind of its own. My body goes through its ups and downs without any regard for my best efforts at making a difference. If healthful living were God, I'd be an atheist by now.

In the past I would get up early in the morning and have my devotions while looking out the window at the sunrise. I don't enjoy that view anymore. My rising time gets later and later. Devotionally, I survive on a subsistence diet most of the time. I grope for texts of comfort here and there in the Word. My prayers keep coming back to the same old problem.

I get upset with God. Sometimes I say (behind His back) that if He wants to communicate with me, He should return my former waking hours. I want the ability to praise Him bright and early again. Instead I get insomnia or my sleep is inexplicably interrupted for three or four hours in the middle of the night. Not stressed out or sick, I'm just wide awake for no earthly reason.

In those hours I've concluded that I will never find a magic bullet. Not any time soon. The only hope I have is that I'll be one of the people who find the affliction goes away after a certain number of years.

But what about right now? I lie awake at night, shuddering to think of my life continuing this way. Chunks of it seem to be sliding by while I'm in bed. Is there a way to use this downtime? I need to do more than think about what I'm losing.

Then one long and depressing night I remembered something about the common cold.

"They can land a man on the moon, but they can't find a cure for the common cold" is a frequent lament—usually made by those coughing and sneezing their way to work. But recently I learned that the common cold or the common flu doesn't have any cure precisely because the symptoms are the cure.

Why does your nose run? Because fluids in your nasal passages and larynx have built up to do battle with antibodies.

Why do you have a fever? Because the heat produced by your body is marshaling its defenses, working overtime to turn back the tide of foreign invaders.

Why do you feel tired? Because your body is trying to conserve energy so it can concentrate on the task at hand: curing your common cold or flu.

Since the era of magic pills and miraculous medicine began, we've developed the idea that the symptoms are the problem. Blast something up that stuffy nose. Spray something down that scratchy throat. Take a couple of aspirin to get rid of the fever. Then head off to work.

We keep attacking the symptoms instead of cooperating with the body's vigorous attempts to set things right. What we really mean when we say there's no cure for the common cold is that we know of no instant solution, no magic bullet that will short-circuit the annoying process of getting well. Instead, we just want the cold to go away so we can go on about our business.

After years of searching for the magic bullet that would end my bout with chronic fatigue, I started thinking that maybe the symptoms are the cure for me too. Maybe my body is just telling me, "Sorry, there is something a little screwy about the immune system in here, and it takes more effort to do what we used to do automatically."

So I started going to bed earlier and sleeping in a little later. And I began regarding my additional rest as the cure as opposed to the problem. And what do you know—I haven't crashed for several months! I'm able to function steadily without having to stay in bed for two to three weeks straight. Watching less TV at night isn't such a big sacrifice. I'm resting more each day. It adds up to fewer waking hours, but I don't feel like an invalid anymore. I'm functioning almost like a well person.

WHAT'S GOOD FOR THE BODY . . .

My struggle with insomnia has given me time to think about more than physical wellness. That uneasy sense of my life slipping away applies to spirituality, too. Enduring my turn at the midlife crisis, I've started to feel intense longings that used to be only in the background. It's a restlessness of the spirit that's every bit as real as my physical frustrations.

I remember what it was like to be close to God, to be part of an exciting movement of the Spirit. But now it sometimes seems as though I'm just tipping my hat to Him from a distance. I feel a yearning for more to life than just this. After years of living a "well-adjusted Christian life" I suddenly realize I'm starving for spiritual intimacy.

And then it hits me—hey, maybe what's true for the body is true for the heart and soul as well—the symptoms are the cure. Perhaps all my longings are a part of the cure. Maybe even the gnawing frustration and the sense of inertia are the way God stirs up our souls and gets us to respond to Him again. God uses the anguish itself to deepen our hearts.

The problem is that it's easier to reach for a magic bullet than to submit to the process of getting well. We want to attack the symptoms. Spray some convenient platitude over that chronic yearning. Blast that scratchiness deep in your heart with some good clean fun. Above all, take regular doses of a busy schedule in order to keep that anguish down.

We just don't have time for the symptoms. That's one big reason so few of us find our way to intimacy with God. It takes time and has no shortcuts. Most of us avoid God not because we're terribly evil or because we have something against Him. Instead, we just can't seem to find the time.

I think that's why God carved a giant stop sign in the rock of Mount Sinai. The fourth commandment, written on stone tablets by the finger of God, tells us to stop on the Sabbath, to halt our frantic pace, to let go of our compulsive "doing," and to spend time with Him.

The fourth commandment comes as the climax of the first three. How do we "have no other gods" before us? How do we bow down to Him alone? How do we reverence His name? We have to give Him the one thing we keep holding back: our time.

Psalm 46:10 sums up the fourth commandment nicely: "Be still, and know that I am God."

Our hearts can best deepen in stillness. We've got to keep a Sabbath in our lives, to take the time to really listen to the "still, small voice." Only God can work the symptoms into a cure.

God promises to come near to the broken in heart, to bind up our wounds. But we keep trying to tape our hearts together before the cracks show. We want to medicate away the symptoms. But the symptoms are meant to take us somewhere. If we repress them too quickly, we never really begin the process of getting well.

AN INVOLUNTARY SABBATH REST

A secular businessperson in Bucharest thought he was having the time of his life. Young and good-looking, Richard had plenty of money to spend in flashy bars and cabarets, plenty of money to spend on the girls of "Little Paris," as people called the city. He was on a fast track through the downtown nightlife. "I didn't care what happened," Richard said, "as long as my appetite for fresh sensation was fed."

Richard left behind him a trail of broken hearts. But it felt so good to have no serious responsibilities. Other young men in his office envied Richard's reputation as a playboy.

True, sometimes he did feel he was throwing away something inside him that was good and useful. Occasionally he even wished that God existed so life could have some meaning. But such moments were few and far between, because he was too busy having fun to worry about the sickness in his soul. He just kept on his fast track, rushing from one party to another, trying to ignore the symptoms.

But then Richard experienced a big dose of Sabbath rest. It wasn't by choice. A serious case of tuberculosis laid him flat on his back for months. He had a lot of time to think in the sanitarium. And that still small voice became audible. The symptoms began leading him somewhere.

At one point Richard prayed, "God, I know You don't exist, but if by some chance You do, it is for You to reveal Yourself to me."

During his convalescence in a mountain village, someone gave him a Bible. He began to read the Gospels. And in the quietness and tranquillity of his enforced Sabbath rest, the young atheist found himself drawn irresistibly to Christ. As he described it: "I could not help comparing Christ's life with mine. His outlook was so pure, mine so tainted; His nature so selfless, mine so greedy; His heart so full of love, mine filled with rancor. My old certainties began to crumble in the face of this wisdom and truthfulness."

Soon Richard Wurmbrand had made a complete commitment to Christ as his Saviour. He finally found time enough to get well, physically and spiritually. And the former playboy went on to become one of Romania's most courageous pastors during the years of Communist oppression.

A LIGHT IN THE DARKNESS

Chronic fatigue syndrome has become a kind of Sabbath rest for me. It's not something I would choose, any more than Pastor Wurmbrand would have chosen tuberculosis. But after years of thrashing in between the sheets and fretting over my persistent physical symptoms, I've started listening more carefully to the symptoms in my heart. During sleepless hours I've felt anguish and yearning. At times they seem to be ripping me apart.

But they are symptoms that slowly lead to a cure if I can set my mind on the Great Physician. I've started using insomnia instead of just trying to get through it. Instead of moaning over the fact that my long hours in bed have erased any chance of an early-morning quiet time, why not have devotions in the middle of the night? God is accessible then, too.

It isn't easy. My thoughts don't naturally stand at attention in praise when I attempt to address God. During that hazy space between honest wakefulness and actual sleep, they often wander away. I have to keep calling them back like restless schoolchildren.

But when I do manage to focus on Christ, it's amazing what can happen. I find myself irresistibly drawn to Him. It's my privilege to stand before Him. He's the one who turned a night darker than mine, the night of a man born blind, into blazing midday color.

Jesus knows all about the darkness. His voice carried through the gloom of Lazarus' tomb, and the corpse walked out into broad daylight. That's Jesus, all right.

Jesus knew about anguish and isolation. He felt the weight of human cruelty crushing His life out at Gethsemane. Suffocated by a vast night, with the disciples snoring a few feet away, He submitted to the Father's will and gave Himself up for us. Jesus knows all about reaching out in the dark.

It was terribly dark in the garden tomb too. Calloused hands had snuffed out the Light of the world. Broken and bled white, His limp body lay on cold stone. He seemed condemned to some outer darkness beyond even the grace of the heavenly Father, forsaken by the One who never forsakes.

But nothing could keep Him in the dark for long. With all the jagged force of an earthquake, a dazzling light ripped through the rock. That broken body transformed itself into a body of light. Soldiers fled. The Light of the world was turned on again.

His was a night far thicker than mine, His body more broken. But He triumphed over it all.

If I can just concentrate long enough to tap into a little praise, thoughts like these build their own momentum. Jesus keeps drawing me. Before, I was lying wide awake at 2:00 a.m. for no earthly reason. But now I've got something to think about. Christ doesn't seem so far away in the stillness.

And I find that my symptoms, my frustration, and my longing have made more room inside me. The prayers that I manage in this limbo strike more deeply. My struggle with this sense of spiritual loss has given my acts of devotion a sharper edge.

What's more, getting into praise is the best way I've found to go to sleep. I don't always succeed in making my midnight devotional, but when I do, it almost always leads to rest. And it's not the unsettled sleep of a man alone with chronic fatigue syndrome, but that of someone who feels arms holding him in the dark.

Chapter Thirteen

Pouring It All Out

Everyone always thought of Yasuko as the perfect child. Relatives and neighbors who dropped by the Tadashi household never heard her complain or whine or beg for things. Always helpful to her mother, she seemed mature beyond her years and took on responsibilities well. When saying goodbye after a visit, Yasuko's aunts would usually pat her on the head and say what a brave little girl she was, growing up without a father, never being a burden on her mother.

Yasuko's dad had died shortly after World War II, when she was only 2. Mr. Tadashi was a wonderful man whom many years later Yasuko would come to admire from stories told by his devoted business associates. After becoming aware that he had contracted a terminal illness, Yasuko's father worked hard at his company and managed to leave his family a sizable sum. But after his death, a certain relative, whose problem with alcohol and poor business sense mixed ominously, had talked Yasuko's mother into investing the savings in a venture that proved disastrous.

So Mrs. Tadashi had to earn a living on her own—no easy task in postwar Japan. She became a teacher of koto, the traditional stringed instrument that young women of good breeding were expected to study. For much of the year Mrs. Tadashi had to teach in the southern island of Kyushu. Yasuko and her sister stayed with their grandmother.

Through all this, Yasuko tried hard to act the part of the perfect child. She was aware of her mother's struggle to support two little girls alone and tried hard not to be a burden. The child learned not to ask for things and always remained the brave little girl in difficult circumstances. Handicapped by her own childhood deprivations, her mother remained distant during those years—emotionally as well as physically. The grandmother had given her away to an aunt when she was 4 years old. The wounds that resulted from the break in the bonding process repeated themselves in the next generation.

A SWEET-SOUNDING PLEA

Fast-forward a few decades to southern California. Yasuko had now become a wife and the happy mother of two children. Like most kids, hers occasionally whined and begged for things they wanted. And like most parents, she and her husband tried to keep it to a minimum. But Yasuko sensed in their plaintive voices something her husband did not. She heard the sound of a child who can ask a parent for anything, the sound of a child secure enough to plead. It was a language she could never learn in her formative years. She could never come freely and comfortably to Dad or Mom and just pour out the desires of her heart.

So even though as a mother Yasuko had to decide carefully what the kids could and could not get by begging, there was comfort as well as discomfort for her in the sometimes shrill sound of their pleas. She was listening to the echo of an innocent, spontaneous language that she, in a different time and place, might have spoken herself.

I believe this is one language we all need to learn in order to recapture a sense of intimacy with God. We need to be able to respond to hardship and misfortune by pouring out our hearts to Him. A stiff upper lip and stoic resolve can be useful at times, but sometimes they prevent us from speaking the language of the heart.

We can trace this distinct language throughout the Psalms. Their tone and cadence suggest a child coming before a parent and pouring it all out. The Psalms cry out for help. Pleas for rescue fill 41 of them. The verses tumble out directly and simply—"Help me; I'm in trouble." We see people appealing to God, often desperately, in all kinds of situations.

As you first read through the Psalms, such cries for help may repulse you. They can start to sound like so much whining. And anyway, it's not often that we find ourselves hounded by the vicious enemies who so heavily populate the book.

But it's important to remember that the Psalms reflect centuries of Israel's history. They highlight momentous occasions in the lives of the Hebrew people. Human beings most often compose great prayers in times of crisis. That's when we come to God most earnestly. The remarkable thing is how often the psalmists' cries for help turn into sounds of praise, even in the worst of circumstances.

We find still another reason for the 41 urgent appeals recorded in the Psalms. God is simply telling us that it's OK to ask. We can come to Him as freely as a child running to a parent. While we may not always ask for the right things, and God will not always answer us in the way we demand, He still invites us to come to Him with our requests. We can speak the innocent, spontaneous language of children secure in their parents' unconditional acceptance.

Some believers have grown up in the faith in a manner not unlike that experienced by Yasuko. Always seeking to live up to the high expectations of the religious "relatives" around them, they try so hard to look good by certain external standards. Not wanting to be a burden on God, they never come pleading for things like other "immature" children of the Father. Instead, they stand up straight (on their own) and follow the divine Example (at a distance).

Becoming more like our Father is certainly a big part of the Christian life. The language of obedience is important for us to learn. But that process will harden into legalism unless we also learn another language: "Please . . ." "I need . . ."

Before we become anything else, we are needy children, totally dependent on our parents. It is true at the beginning of physical life, at the beginning of spiritual life, and at the start of every day of our Christian life. The Psalms show us that it's good to be secure enough to plead at the feet of the Father who cherishes us.

Coming to God as vulnerable children is one more way in which our hearts deepen. By becoming transparent in our need, we allow the Father to stretch us, to make more room in us for Himself. It's not the beauty but the honesty of our prayers that counts. Intimacy requires honesty. Can we come to God in our lowest moments? That's the question misfortune pushes at us.

The Psalms give us plenty of examples of a painful honesty. They show us people pouring their hearts out in all kinds of trying circumstances, reminding us it's not only OK to plead for help but also to ask why.

The Psalms are, by definition, vehicles of praise to the God of heaven. Yet they often begin in a highly unexalted state. The anguished question "Why?" finds an echo throughout the Psalms.

Elsewhere Scripture assures that our heavenly Father will never leave us or forsake us. But the psalmists give voice to the unthinkable:

"My God, my God, why have you forsaken me?" (Ps. 22:1).

They even accuse God of being absent when needed most:

"Why, O Lord, do you stand far off? Why do you hide yourself in times of trouble?" (Ps. 10:1).

"Awake, O Lord! Why do you sleep?
    Rouse yourself! Do not reject us forever.
    Why do you hide your face
    and forget our misery and oppression?" (Ps. 44:23, 24).
"O Lord God Almighty,
    how long will your anger smolder
    against the prayers of your people?" (Ps. 80:4).

Obviously the Psalms are not just pretty pictures of God—they also give voice to our deepest human feelings. We hear cries of desperation, lostness, perplexity, sorrow . . . even terrible rage. Such prayers come straight from the heart. They are not always dressed in their Sabbath best.

Sometimes we even read things that are a bit shocking. Some psalms, for example, urge God to blot certain disreputable people out of the book of life, or to dash the infants of the pagans against the rocks.

Scholars have gone to great lengths to explain the imprecatory psalms as stylized, formal, judicial statements that are quite different from your run-of-the-mill hateful letter. Undoubtedly that has some truth, but I see a more important point made through these jagged shouts. It is simply this: God listens. We can come to Him and spill out whatever is on our hearts because He listens.

Here is perhaps the first thing we all need to know about God: He is willing to listen to us no matter what we have to say. He doesn't respond only when we have composed an appropriately pious prayer, but opens His ears and His heart when we are feeling depressed, when we can't think of one nice thing to say about so-and-so, when we are mad enough to eat nails, when we aren't even sure He cares or is even there at all.

The Psalms are not always about God speaking—sometimes they are about God listening. Yet the overwhelming majority do express sentiments that are directly inspiring. Only six psalms focus exclusively on getting even with personal enemies. Many more, of course, express personal devotion to God. And although several psalms reflect despair almost from beginning to end, about three times as many present desperate cries for help mixed with expressions of faith.

Clearly God wants us to move from a fixation on our problems or enemies to a steady gaze at Himself. But Scripture records a few unedited, unsanitized, unsanctified prayers as well. And they are there for a reason—to show us that God listens from the very start. He hears our prayers before we can even pray in faith, listens to our anger before we can focus it constructively.

God is a good listener. That we can come to Him with our most intimate secrets and feelings is an important theme in the Psalms that we often overlook. Those sometimes ragged, heated cries tell us that it's OK to ask why or to feel bad. God is listening.

SEARCHING FOR COMFORT

I was spending another evening in the bedroom with only my reading light for company instead of joining the rest of the family watching TV. My own emotional turmoil felt too intense to allow room for any artificial drama. I'd hit a brick wall in my marriage. Looking back over the crisis my wife had been going through, I could see only the times she'd been dumping on me, blaming me. Burned out, I couldn't say "I'm sorry" anymore. I didn't want to understand— I just wanted another life.

All the anger that had been building for months threatened to come out in raging speeches. My protests seemed to circle round and round me in the dark room, gathering momentum as I saw more and more reasons to be resentful.

"How does she expect me to be supportive when she is attacking me? No matter what I do, it will never be good enough. I will never make her feel loved. I can't ever fill up the holes in her heart. And she considers her pain and anger always my fault."

At the same time these imprecations were spilling out of me, I felt more intensely aware of my need for love than at any other time in my life. I circled my defenses and argued my case in my own mind, feeling totally empty. As I stared at the ceiling, catching bursts of TV dialogue drifting up from the family room, I knew how terrible it is to be alone with that one-track inner voice.

So I started pouring all my ugliness out to God—this is how I feel; here's all the garbage. And as I prayed, my arguments turned into simple cries for help. I couldn't concentrate on how terrible I felt my wife was. My own need loomed too large, my own emptiness echoed too loudly. All I could do was spread out my sorry self before the Lord, and He didn't seem terribly interested in who was right.

Then, taking my Bible down from the headboard shelf, I reached for another voice. I had opened the Bible many times before—to study a topic, to do research for a writing project, to have a quiet time. But this was different. I wasn't just grasping at truth, I was reaching for a companion. I felt that if someone else didn't reach out to me there in that room, I would suffocate in my own spinning emotions.

Flipping through various Epistles I caught familiar phrases about grace and love. Finally I glanced through John and stopped at Jesus' encounter with the woman at the well. Something about the way He extended Himself by asking for a favor rang a bell. His gracious way of touching this outcast's need made me pause and admire. Suddenly I had something else to look at.

The same thing happened to me again during subsequent evenings alone with my reading light in the bedroom. The Word proved a good companion. It gave me a way to get out of myself when I desperately needed to do so. A very different kind of voice, it told me that God was listening, that He was very close.

I don't think it's a coincidence that I experience this kind of intimacy during my most vulnerable moments. I had laid out my crushed heart before God and found that He could deepen it considerably. He made room for more of Himself.

God does come close to the vulnerable. Almost all those psalms that offer up cries of anguish also present praise for eventual rescue. If many of the psalms reflect deeply wounded hearts, many also speak of deeply felt healing. The psalmists confidently praise the God who "heals the brokenhearted and binds up their wounds" (Ps. 147:3). These writers speak from experience when they declare:

"The Lord is close to the brokenhearted
   and saves those who are crushed in spirit" (Ps. 34:18).

Yes, God knows all about pain and rejection. He doesn't stand aloof as we suffocate in our overwhelming emotions. God knows all about being cut off from those closest to Him, all about suffering unjustly.

Can God touch our pain? Yes, He already has—all of it. He knows what it's like to be a victim. Absorbing the guilt of child molesters, thieves, rapists, abusive parents, warmongers, drug pushers—He took it all on Himself at Golgotha. On the cross all these tragedies and all this pain crushed Jesus beneath its weight.

The fact that God listens can lead us to great healing. And it all starts when we pour out our hearts like children running into our father's arms.

WHERE IS GOD?

The early sun cast long shadows as Asaph walked east through Jerusalem toward the tent of meeting. He'd told his wife he was going to polish the Temple cymbals, but mostly he wanted to be alone this morning. Asaph was facing a personal crisis of faith. A chronic illness was wearing him down. Some musicians at the Temple were misusing their position of trust. Tragedy had struck his home. And God seemed unconcerned about it all.

As Asaph walked along he passed the houses of rich merchants who treated the law of God with contempt. He knew of some who'd even sold fellow Hebrews into slavery, leaving their families destitute. How was it that the wicked could prosper so conspicuously?

Since childhood Asaph had absorbed the teachings contained in the ark that King David had, with great celebration, brought up to the tent of meeting.

The covenant was enshrined there—Deuteronomy's litany of blessings and cursings. It had assured Israel that the righteous would be blessed, that the Lord would open His storehouse in heaven for them. But the wicked would be cursed, struck with wasting disease, with blight and drought. The sky would turn to bronze above them, the earth to iron.

But if this was the case, God didn't seem to be paying attention to His own promises. Dark thoughts raced through Asaph's head. Did God indeed see everything? Had He overlooked the depredations of evil people? Had He also ignored the struggles of all the impoverished who called on His name?

The remarkable testimony that David's musician/poet Asaph has left us in Psalm 73 relates to a time in the man's life when he almost gave in to despair. The question "Why?" loomed over him as large and ominous as a beast from the apocalypse. A God of righteous blessings clashed irreconcilably with the obvious injustices of the world. Why did He allow such things? This psalm is not so much an appeal for comfort as a plea for a real answer, something that makes sense on a personal level.

One of the reasons misfortunes can deepen our hearts is that they force us to ask specific questions. Seeking and asking, we search for a specific response spoken only in the language of our hearts. It's good to have the comfort from knowing that God listens to us. But we need His answers even more.

Asaph tells us in Psalm 73 that the lights went on for him when he "entered the sanctuary of God." Once he realized that God had been by his side all along, he found a way out of his despair. Even when Asaph had been wildly ranting and raving, God had been taking it all in sympathetically and had begun to guide him to an answer.

> "I was senseless and ignorant;
>> I was a brute beast before you.
>> Yet I am always with you;
>> you hold me by my right hand" (Ps. 73:22, 23).

Somewhere in that Temple courtyard Asaph said to himself: "Even if I never get much in the way of a material quality of life, I will still have known the God who is my portion forever. Isn't having a relationship with Him worth more in the balance than all the riches unscrupulous people can boast of?"

As the light dawned on him in the sanctuary, Asaph came to the point of affirming with some enthusiasm:

"Whom have I in heaven but you?
And being with you, I desire nothing on earth" (verse 25).

The man grew content as he contemplated what he now knew to be the bottom line in his life: "It is good to be near God."

Asaph received to his question "Why?" an answer that satisfied him on an emotional level. He found an insight that silenced his personal cry of anguish.

And often that's what we need too. Sometimes those logical answers don't do us much good. When the person down the street gets lung cancer, answers on an intellectual level are usually enough for us. We can understand why evil has broken out on our planet and is running its course. But when a loved one gets leukemia, we need an answer on an emotional level. The concept of an overall plan for the universe isn't enough. Talk about the "larger view" has a hollow echo. We want God to answer this particular "Why?" We want an answer that reaches our broken hearts.

TUNING IN TO THE LANGUAGE OF THE HEART

The Psalms tell us that God does indeed give us such answers. We find Him in the darkest pits, hear a voice that breaks an opening in even the darkest horizon-to-horizon gloom. Many psalms are testimonies to that effect.

But here's the catch. To receive answers on an emotional level you have to become a good listener. Soul-satisfying insights don't come in the form of notes from heaven that we can casually pick up at a post office box. We have to listen carefully for them in those places that God chooses to reveal them.

Thankfully, God models such important behavior for us. He listens intently as we pour out our hearts—as if each person is the only one in the universe speaking to Him. God can give us that kind of attention, and He inspires a similar receptivity in return. We need to give God our full attention in prayer, to listen carefully, if we are to hear the language that speaks to our hearts.

When overwhelmed by despair, Asaph felt tempted to go in two directions, both leading away from listening. First he says his feet almost slipped (Ps. 73:2)—he nearly lost his spiritual foothold. That is, he almost decided that efforts to keep his heart pure were all "in vain." If things are a mess, why not sin a little and get something pleasurable out of it all?

That's a natural response to perplexity. We often loosen up our moral lifestyle in direct proportion to how unsure we become about God's truth. Hedging our bets, in a sense, we don't want to make any great sacrifices if heaven is anything less than a sure thing. Rarely is it a conscious choice—it is more often something we drift into.

However, slipping into sin and listening to God don't go together. Trying to do both creates internal conflict. Something has to give. That's why we try to keep God at arm's length when we are indulging in shady activities. We give Scripture a cursory glance, toss the Lord a quick greeting in the morning, or avoid spiritual practices altogether.

But Asaph was not willing to do that. He had to keep hearing his Lord up close and personal. He would not react to perplexity by sinning—getting back at God by wandering off from the straight and narrow.

In order to prevent times of anguish from pushing us off into transgression, we must decide to keep talking and to keep listening. Answers that satisfy our hearts come through God's still small voice, not some quick little sin.

The other pitfall Asaph faced in his time of trial was bitterness. Yet when that attitude began to sink in—"my heart was grieved and my spirit embittered" (verse 21)—he didn't mope about the house and nourish those feelings. Instead, he went to the Temple.

Every loss we experience in life requires a certain amount of mourning. Sadness is a normal, healthy response to the bad things that happen. It turns to bitterness only when we rehearse the loss again and again to ourselves—and find no outlet for the sorrow. Asaph dealt with the problem of bitterness by opening up to God. Although much of what he said in the beginning may have seemed nothing but ugliness, he kept talking and kept listening. By pouring out his feelings to the Father, he prevented them from hardening into the mind-set that life is the pits and God doesn't care.

We become bitter when we stop listening to God and insist on wallowing in our own pain. Thus we need to find a way out—not by ignoring our feelings, but by laying them before God and attempting to be what He is: a good listener. No matter what feelings we bring to the Father, if we give Him time He will speak to us in a language that satisfies the heart.

LEARNING TO LET GO

During those evenings alone in my bedroom I heard that language and found that God could do more than listen—He could also answer. He could instruct as well as comfort.

One particularly dark night my spinning emotions pushed me down to a new low. I could see only the times my wife and I hadn't connected in our marriage. And it seemed that I was stuck in a relationship that had no morally acceptable way out.

The bed felt as wide and empty as a tundra. The mirror on the opposite wall threw back a hollow, yellow face. Outside our window our dog barked at the coyotes on the dry sagebrush hills above our house, as if echoing all my loneliness and animosity.

In that moment I knew the only thing that counted in life was emotional intimacy. Everything else was just a means to that end. And I felt sure I would never be able to experience that kind of closeness with my wife. It just wouldn't happen.

In my emotional limbo I'd been fantasizing about other women. It was all too easy to imagine instant emotional intimacy with them, easy to picture them as giving and open and deep. The more I thought about it, though, the more horrified I became. But the possibility of spending the rest of my life in a marriage without emotional intimacy was unbearable. I was really suffocating now.

Although I knew clearly what my moral obligations were, keeping my vows appeared like a kind of suicide. The long-term prospects seemed too grim to think about, yet I couldn't stop dwelling on them.

Again I needed help in the worst way. And I reached for the Word again like a man reaches for a lifeline before going down for the third time. As I opened Scripture I laid it all out before the Lord—I needed a reason not to throw everything away that very minute.

An answer came: "Delight yourself in the Lord and he will give you the desires of your heart" (Ps. 37:4). I had been agonizing over the terrible alternatives facing me—give up my most important commitment, or abandon all hope of emotional intimacy. But God nudged me away from this false dilemma. "You don't have to try to hack off this part of you that longs for intimacy," He spoke quietly to me. "Just commit yourself to fulfilling that desire only in God's way. Trust Me. Delight in My will. That's your job. My job is to satisfy the deepest desires of your heart. I'll enable you to experience intimacy in some way."

With both hands I grabbed hold of this slice of hope. Yes, delighting myself in the Lord was definitely better than being emotionally lost in the darkness. Soon other bits of Scripture came along to fill in the picture.

One of Jesus' great axioms seemed aimed right at my forehead: "Whoever finds his life will lose it, and whoever loses his life for my sake will find it" (Matt. 10:39). James also hit a bull's-eye: "Every good and perfect gift is from above, coming down from the Father of the heavenly lights, who does not change like shifting shadows" (James 1:17).

Lying there with only the Word to fend off the enormous emotional storm raging around me, I suddenly grew quite confident. Yes, I knew beyond a shadow of a doubt that if I gave up my demand for emotional intimacy for Christ's sake—that is, if I refused to follow my fantasies and seek intimacy outside of His will—then I would find what I was longing for. But if I grabbed for immediate emotional intimacy, trying to make it happen on my own, then it would surely slip through my fingers.

It wasn't some nice but abstract principle that I acknowledged dutifully. At that moment Jesus' words became as real to me as the law of gravity. Their truth sank into my bones. And I echoed James' affirmation: yes, every perfect gift, every gift worth having, is His alone to give. Intimacy will happen within my commitment to follow the will of the Father. Nothing of value will come to me from outside God's will. The path to intimacy goes through God and leads to abundance. Everything else is a compromise, no matter how dazzling it may appear from a distance.

I had my answer, my way out of the storm. It was as clear as a shaft of light cutting through the clouds. As I dozed off that night, it didn't just seem like I'd stumbled on a fortuitous truth, but as if I'd been dialoguing with God Himself.

I'd called out desperately with a very specific dilemma. And He had answered just as specifically.

I didn't know for sure whether the marriage could be saved or not. But I knew that I could not end it by doing something dishonorable.

One of the main reasons we can experience intimacy with God is that He answers us intimately. A sense of dialogue makes us feel close to Him. It's wonderful when the Father responds to our personal need with a passage from Scripture that turns on the lights. I've seen it happen on many occasions. I experience real dialogue with God when I'm genuinely looking for an answer. Real answers usually don't tumble down as we randomly place a finger on some text. Yet they do come when we pour out our hearts to the God who listens so well. They do come when we listen carefully to the God who still speaks impressively through His Word.

Chapter Fourteen

To Surrender and to Resist

Does it ever seem to you that misfortunes come in clusters, that they're never nicely spaced out? I felt that during a recent financial crunch.

First, an issue of the magazine I edit was canceled.

Then a television series I'd been working on was postponed. I'd done a lot of research, checking out locations in London, Amsterdam, and Prague. But all the planning time I'd already invested suddenly became unbillable.

Worst of all, my major client, facing budget constraints, informed me the company would have to limit the number of scripts contracted per year—and I'd already passed my quota. But the year still had three more months to go. Suddenly the well had dried up. How was I going to support my family? I could acknowledge by faith that the Lord would take care of us one way or another. But emotionally, it felt as though the walls were closing in. All the bad things were happening at once.

One of our biggest challenges, when trials bowl us over, is simply to keep from letting them imprison us. When misfortunes hit us hard we feel we're no longer in control. Sometimes it seems as though bad things constantly keep us off balance. We're never able to really get our lives together, never able to build up any momentum as we work toward our goals.

So far in this section we've talked about allowing God to use symptoms (the anguish and longing) to cure us, about pouring our hearts out to God and listening for answers that speak to our hearts. We've concentrated on our internal response to trials. But what about our external reaction? What can we offer in reply to difficulties? God has promised to refashion misfortunes into something useful. How can we cooperate so we are not just mangled, but actually molded into a better shape?

SURRENDERING THE CITY

Two prisoners in the Bible modeled two vital responses to misfortune. Both individuals knew a lot about trouble. And their behavior in the worst of times shows us how the process of letting God mold us can deepen the heart and build intimacy.

Jeremiah was a man who knew about trouble. For him, the city of Jerusalem had become a prison that constantly threatened him. Here's a partial list of what he endured.

● Pashhur, the chief officer in the Temple, had Jeremiah beaten and placed in stocks (Jer. 20).

● Priests and prophets dragged him before King Jehoiakim's magistrates, demanding capital punishment. A few "elders of the land" interceded and managed to save his life (Jer. 26).

● During a time of siege, King Zedekiah threw Jeremiah into a dungeon in which he almost died. God's prophet had to beg for his life. At the last minute the authorities sent him to the courtyard of the guard and gave him a ration of bread (Jer. 37).

● When Jeremiah still wouldn't be silenced, several officials had him lowered by ropes into a well. He sank into the mud. A Cushite in the royal palace, fearing Jeremiah would starve to death, arranged for the prophet's release back to the courtyard (Jer. 38).

Yes, Jeremiah knew about affliction. But even more trying than the physical abuse he endured was the isolation that gnawed at his bones. His was a lonely moral voice in a time of almost universal apostasy. Alone, he cried out against corruption and injustice until the hoarseness reached down into his heart. Jeremiah anguished over his calling. He wanted so much to stop pleading with the indifferent, to stop kicking at the brick wall. But God wouldn't let him. The prophetic fire in his belly burned on, and it seemed to Jeremiah that he had to speak or die.

Jeremiah's troubles really center on one message. Everything in his long book moves to a climax to it. Through the whole narrative we observe a running skirmish between his irrepressible "Thus says the Lord" and Judah's decadence. The conflict comes to a head in chapter 21. The Babylonians have surrounded Jerusalem again—Nebuchadnezzar is out for more conquests. Prophets for hire have been mouthing their cheap good news that God will surely rescue His people and destroy Babylon.

But Jeremiah, as usual, lays out the cold truth from his Lord: "See, I am setting before you the way of life and the way of death. Whoever stays in this city will die by the sword, famine or plague. But whoever goes out and surrenders to the Babylonians who are besieging you will live; he will escape with his life" (Jer. 21:8, 9).

To the Jews, the chosen people of God, these could only be the words of a traitor. The people of Jerusalem figured Jeremiah must be palming shekels from Nebuchadnezzar. A prophet of Yahweh urging the abandonment of the holy city? Impossible. Surely God would allow no pagan hand to touch the Most Holy Place.

For some time Jeremiah had been proclaiming that unless the people turned back to the Lord, Judah would have to submit to His chastening through the Babylonians. The Jewish leaders had steadfastly resisted his message. Zion was sacred—nothing would ever change that fact. Quoting Scripture to back up their point, they reminded him that they were the chosen people and nothing could change that. Calls to surrender their Temple to the enemy seemed sheer blasphemy.

In this moment of truth for a besieged city I see one of the most basic struggles we face in our lives. Each of us is instinctively a fortress. Our ego quickly defends its turf. Any challenge to our sense of self feels like a battering ram against us. Nothing, it seems, could be clearer than that the criticisms and irritations that besiege us are wrong. The trials that haunt us surely must be unjust. How can God allow them to touch us?

Think about it. What's our first reaction when bad things happen? We fight back. After hearing the bad news from my major client, I came home with an attitude. "They want to *limit* the number of scripts I write. Can you believe these people? Don't they realize what a brilliant writer I am? How invaluable my services are? Don't I have a *right* to keep producing as much as I can?"

Jerusalem represents comfort and the familiar. It's inertia, security. We don't want to let go of our habits or deal with our problems—even though they may cause us to starve spiritually. So we hunker down behind the walls.

But Jeremiah gives us an alternative. Don't promise to tidy up the streets or buttress a few walls, he says. Leave the city. Don't mess with the self and all its defenses, just abandon it.

The message for us in the book of Jeremiah is to surrender the city. It makes everything fit together. Jeremiah's heavy words about unwashable stains, incurable wounds, stubborn hearts, false peace, adulterous idolatry, cruel oppression, and innocent blood spilled all shake the ground underneath the city. They lead up to a call to surrender.

Jeremiah's bright pictures of wounds healed, health restored, the yoke of slavery broken, a law written on the heart, and a Righteous Branch ruling with justice and righteousness all relate to the city after surrender. They advertise a wonderful armistice.

Sometimes misfortunes expose a problem in our lives or bad things on the outside point to something we need to deal with on the inside. That's the way it was with Judah. They had a chronic problem. You might call it the compulsive bowing problem. Ashtoreth, Baal, Chemosh—they never met an idol they didn't like. God's people failed again and again to root out the high places of idolatry in their midst.

Nebuchadnezzar's latest conquest had finally exposed their weakness. As a matter of fact, the trauma of the Babylonian captivity did force the Hebrews to deal with their problem. Never again did idolatry plague them.

That's why when misfortune exposes a problem in our lives we need to respond with that white flag above the city and surrender.

"I'VE GOT PEACE LIKE A RIVER . . ."

My previous computer had a distressing habit of freezing up at the worst possible moment. I'd be almost finished with a telecast script, would try to save the document, then . . . crash! The machine would become paralyzed. I couldn't move the cursor, and would punch every key but nothing happened. The only way to get the program going again was to turn the computer off. But that meant losing everything I'd been working on.

I would have to rewrite an entire chapter or script. And the more I had to work to re-create what I had just written, the more indignant I'd get. With every keystroke I would protest, "I shouldn't have to do this."

When the material was slow in coming back to me, I'd often blow up and pound on the desk. What I really wanted to do was punch the screen out and teach that demon-possessed word processor a lesson. But that would have been too costly of an exorcism. So I settled for a little ranting.

Then one day my erratic computer managed to make a point instead of just trouble. As I reconstructed the lost script, I fumed about all the time that had gone down the drain. It happened to have been a script about the peace of God flowing into one's life. Suddenly I caught myself banging away at the keys, typing furiously about how remarkable God's peace is.

The irony finally got through to me. I was trying to expound wonderful religious principles and spit nails at the same time. Instead I needed to surrender. I caught a glimpse of Jeremiah's white flag flying above the city.

Misfortune will imprison us as long as we keep protesting that it shouldn't have happened. We have to accept the fact that bad things do strike everybody and that God is eager to use that adversity for our benefit.

Surrendering when misfortune strikes means that we say, "OK, Lord, I'm willing to deal with my problem, my unhealthy response." The kind of trials that require our surrender usually involve the petty annoyances of life, the little things that make us angry or resentful. Instead of just pounding away at the obstacle, we take responsibility for our attitudes and emotions. And we ask God to mold us through the unpleasant experience: "Make me more flexible, Lord" or "Make me more forgiving."

When we invest our emotional energy in defending ourselves, we have a hard time experiencing intimacy. When criticism is always a terrible threat, when every inconvenience is a personal affront, then we're just hunkering down inside the walls of our fortress. We may keep some of the pain away, but we also hold God at arm's length.

Surrendering, going out of the city empty-handed, is a step toward intimacy. By placing ourselves in God's hands, we find that it's good to let Him mold us. It's good to stretch. God can use the bad things to make good things happen in our hearts.

But surrender is only part of the story. Not all bad things that happen to us point to some problem we're not dealing with. Random destructive forces lurk out there in the world. Sometimes surrendering to misfortune means giving in to evil, and we need to resist, not surrender.

The Hebrews faced the same dilemma. True, the Babylonian captivity was the strong medicine that finally cured their chronic idolatry, but Babylon was also an aggressive, militaristic empire that would try to swallow up Hebrew faith in its pagan culture. How could God's people resist this toxic side effect—even as they were taking the medicine?

FLYING GOD'S BANNER

Another prisoner gives us an answer. A young Hebrew captive named Daniel also knew about trouble. Taken into exile in Babylon as a young man, he would never again see his beloved homeland. His promising future as a prince of Judah seemed finished as his Babylonian handlers set about to wash his brain of all Hebrew sentiment.

Daniel responded to his misfortune in a remarkable way. His unique method of resisting forms a theme that runs through all his famous adventures.

● The Babylonian authorities tell Daniel and his Hebrew companions that they must eat at the royal table, yet the menu contains foods Levitical law proscribes as unclean. What does Daniel do? He could whisper apologetically to the chief steward, "Uh, listen, we have some peculiar religious customs related to diet. If you could accommodate us . . ."

Instead, he boldly proposes the world's first comparative dietary study. "Please test your servants for ten days: Give us nothing but vegetables to eat and water to drink. Then compare our appearance with that of the young men who eat the royal food, and treat your servants in accordance with what you see" (Dan. 1:12, 13). Daniel is confident that God's way is best and welcomes the chance to prove it. The chief steward agrees to the test and finds, to his surprise, that after

10 days on their simpler diet, the Hebrews do indeed look "healthier and better nourished" than the men who've been indulging in the king's rich fare.

● King Nebuchadnezzar has a highly disturbing dream that he ought to remember but can't. When his wise men can't tell him what it was, he orders their death. What does Daniel do? He prays for divine wisdom and then tells the official executioner, "Take me to the king, and I will interpret his dream for him" (Dan. 2:24). The Hebrew prophet succeeds in reconstructing the king's own forgotten dream. Why? Because "there is a God in heaven."

● Out to trap Daniel, Persian officials sweet-talk King Darius into approving a decree stating that persons who pray to anyone other than him will be cast into a den of lions. What does Daniel do? He opens his window toward Jerusalem and prays to the God of heaven—just as he has always done—three times a day.

In accordance with the law, he gets thrown to the ravenous beasts. Yet he survives a night in their company. Why? Because: "My God sent his angel, and he shut the mouths of the lions" (Dan. 6:22).

Although held captive in a hostile environment, Daniel didn't just try to get by or conform to a pagan culture. He still believed he could fly God's banner in Babylon, demonstrating God's way as best and standing for truth anytime, anywhere.

As a result, Babylon came to know Daniel as the young man with "an extraordinary spirit." And later Belshazzar's queen would say of him: "There is a man in your kingdom who has the spirit of the holy gods in him. . . . And wisdom like that of the gods" (Dan. 5:11).

Daniel shows us that the best way to resist the evil in the bad things that happen to us is not to rail against enemies or to shake our fists at the terrible world. Rather it's to demonstrate an alternative. God's way is still best. I can resist evil by excelling in the qualities that really count and showing that God's principles do work in the worst of circumstances.

A TIME TO RESIST

On February 13, 1943, an official black automobile came to a stop in the French village of Le Chambon. The Vichy—those French who carried out the orders of the Nazis occupying France—had come at last. They'd cut all telephone and telegraph lines, and surrounded the town with armed police squads.

Snow swirled against the cobblestones as Major Silvani stepped out of the car. He knocked on the door of the Protestant presbytery where Pastor Andre Trocme lived. Trocme's wife, Magda, answered. No, her husband wasn't home—he was out visiting parishioners.

What she didn't say was that he was with the Jewish refugees who had been streaming into town for many months. He was out checking on the network of safe houses where they hid.

Solemnly Major Silvani asked to wait for Pastor Trocme. Magda ushered him into the study, knowing the time had come. She always kept a suitcase packed for her husband, filled with clothes and everything she could think he might need in a concentration camp.

Finally the pastor, a large, energetic man, stomped into the house and spotted Major Silvani. After speaking to him for a few moments, he went into the dining room and, holding his wife's shoulders, said, "Magda, I am arrested."

And that's when she remembered that the suitcase was empty. So many refugees, so many scared, lost people had needed those warm clothes.

They stared at each other a moment, then Magda, a very practical woman, rushed off to see what she could put into the suitcase.

After they finished packing, Pastor Trocme and Magda invited Major Silvani to have supper with them. The Vichy policeman was so ashamed that he hardly touched his plate. The pastor, as usual, ate heartily, pausing only to ask why he was being arrested.

"I know nothing. I can say nothing," Silvani replied.

By this time word of the official black car's arrival at the presbytery had gotten out, and the villagers of Le Chambon began arriving to say goodbye to their beloved pastor. They tearfully embraced him, and many pressed packets into his hands—unobtainable things that people keep hidden in wartime: sardines, chocolate biscuits, sausages, warm stockings.

Major Silvani sat in wide-eyed amazement as the table filled with gifts from the poor villagers. Descendants of the Huguenots, they had had to make a big decision when the evil of Nazism swept over their land. They had to decide how to respond when the Vichy government cooperated with the Nazi program of deporting all Jews and other undesirables. The Nazis were capable of wiping out entire villages, massacring those who opposed them.

Under Pastor Trocme's leadership they had decided to fight back—but not in the way the Nazis did. They decided to resist by creating what in the Old Testament was called a city of refuge, a place where people could run for shelter "lest innocent blood be shed."

The Bible study groups that Pastor Trocme had established all over the parish, mostly among the young people, became an underground network, guiding refugees to shelter. All around Le Chambon attics and basements and barns began to fill up with "relatives." People who needed food rations, new identity papers, and a place to hide when the gestapo swept through.

The citizens of Le Chambon determined to preserve the lives of strangers in the face of tyranny. They would create at least one city of refuge.

Of course, eventually the Germans and the Vichy police became suspicious. And that's why Major Silvani had arrived in his black official automobile.

Magda tried to pack as many of the gifts as she could in her husband's suitcase. Then he embraced his daughter and three young boys, not knowing if he would ever see them again.

Major Silvani ushered Pastor Trocme out into the narrow, crooked street toward the automobile. The people of Le Chambon had lined both sides of the street, their wooden shoes (leather ones were long gone) stuck in the snow. They stared at their pastor as he and Major Silvani stepped gingerly over the icy stones. Hidden among the crowd were refugees from all over Central Europe.

Suddenly a voice rang out. And one by one the villagers began to sing, "A Mighty Fortress Is Our God." The hymn grew louder and louder. They closed in behind Pastor Trocme as he passed, their voices echoing off the old town walls, their wooden shoes clop-clopping on the thin snow.

That day Pastor Trocme and two of his colleagues left the city of refuge for a concentration camp. A little later the Nazis deported the inmates of that camp to death camps in Poland and salt mines in Silesia. Almost all died in gas chambers or from hard labor.

But by a remarkable set of circumstances, the authorities released Pastor Trocme and his two friends before the deportation. Afterward, Pastor Trocme continued his work under the noses of the gestapo, sometimes having to flee into the night. Despite the danger, Le Chambon stood against the Nazis and the threat of massacre. In fact, the town became the safest place for Jews in all of France during World War II. To the very end, until the last Nazi soldier fled, it remained unconditionally a city of refuge.

TWO PATHS TO INTIMACY

Two prisoners: Jeremiah and Daniel. Two flags: the flag of surrender and the flag of resistance. Together they show us how we can be free in our hearts even when the walls are closing in. And we need both flags in order for intimacy to grow.

People who always resist when bad things happen—banging against every obstacle, railing at every misfortune—end up resisting God. They never take responsibility for their response to trials or let God use pain to point out something that needs to be fixed in their own lives.

On the other hand, people who always surrender when bad things happen—passively absorbing every blow of fate—end up surrendering to evil. Allowing destructive forces and manipulative people to shape their lives, they don't take responsibility for showing that God's way is best.

No neat formula will tell us exactly when to surrender and when to resist. The important thing is that in both cases we focus on God and not misfortune. We should not surrender to bad things; we should surrender to God, because He uses bad things for our good. Nor should we resist evil by railing against it; instead we should show that God has a better way.

Misfortune can either push us away from God or throw us into His arms. It all depends on the flags we're flying—the flag of surrender or the flag of resistance. They keep us looking up, no matter what the circumstances. We can glorify God in any situation. Nothing can happen to us that He cannot use.

Bad things do come our way. Misfortune sometimes arrives in clusters. And we can go through our whole lives held hostage to frustration and fear. Or we can look up and affirm that no matter what the circumstances, we will honor Christ. Whatever happens, we can experience intimacy with the Lord. Nothing in heaven or earth, no trouble or hardship, can separate me from the nurturing love of God that is in Christ Jesus.

Part Six

A Religion
That Deepens Our Hearts

Chapter Fifteen

Spreading Our Branches

I t took me a long time to find the Church of the Holy Sepulchre, as I wandered all over the narrow winding streets of old Jerusalem. When I finally got inside, I determined to check out the main attraction. A shrine encloses the actual sepulchre site. It's quite small, and you have to crouch to pass through a narrow cavelike entrance. Gold and silver icons and ornaments emblazon everything inside. I wedged into a corner and waited for something to happen. Just the idea of Christ's tomb was quite sobering.

After several minutes of absolute quiet, a crippled man managed to maneuver inside, bent over his crutches. Two boys attended him. The man clutched a sackful of candles and, with great difficulty, got them out of their wrapping and lit each one. As his sons watched solemnly, he set them in a line on the edge of the stone slab covering the tomb.

They stood silently for a moment, and I listened to the father's heavy, uneven breathing. It seemed to carry such a weight of prayer.

Then a priest bustled in. Not in a good mood, he had just reprimanded a tourist for backing into the shrine, a definite insult. He noticed the candles and grunted loudly. They were not all standing straight. A few were even broken. Mumbling something I couldn't understand, he swept the offending candles up in his fist and tossed them in a trash bag. Then he placed the correct ones on the stone, the ones you buy in the cathedral, and lit them carefully while the crippled father stood by with head bowed apologetically.

Job done, the priest bustled out again, leaving us in the dead silence.

A RELIGION OF PETTINESS

One of the great obstacles to intimacy with God can actually be religion, a certain kind of religion that majors in quantities instead of qualities. If we don't aim for spiritual qualities, petty things start to dominate our perspective. When God's deep and wide and broad mercy does not form the center of our faith, superficial things rush in to fill the vacuum. Small things take on an extraordinary importance.

People attack Christmas trees, for example, considering them part of pagan rites that bring the devil into our homes. ·

Some people get offended if others raise their hands in church. Those who haven't cracked a smile in 20 years speak fearfully of unbridled emotionalism.

Projecting song lyrics up on a screen instead of using the hymnal can become a big issue. Horrors, we're turning the church into a night club. Using electronic instruments causes some to waver in their faith.

The wrong candles placed on the edge of the Holy Sepulchre overshadowed the glory of the Resurrection.

SQUEEZING GOD OUT OF OUR RELIGION

Something hit me that day in Jerusalem. This priest, at least at this moment, had degenerated into a janitor. He had everything to say about the proper way to light candles, but absolutely nothing to declare about the wonder of Christ's resurrection. Standing there a few inches from the sepulchre, he had nothing to express about hope or renewal.

One of the reasons so many religious people feel disconnected from God is that He simply can't fit into the confines of their little religion. It just doesn't have enough room. Our minds get stuck on the mechanics of the faith and refuse to let grace broaden them.

At church we may have a lot to say about who has taken up the offering too many times, or not enough times; a lot to say about the bizarre hat Mrs. Murphy refuses to take off; a lot to say about the social committee dragging their feet, or the pastor failing to visit Aunt Bertha. But do we have anything to say about God? Do we want to reflect back to others His wonderful qualities?

If we have nothing to declare about God, we'll always cling to the little stuff. And we will find less and less of God in our religion, because He simply can't cram much of Himself in there.

When in church I'm really admiring something about God, then I can praise Him even through nineteenth-century hymns that talk about billows of love and hearts with rapture thrilled. But if I have nothing to say, then I'll probably spend the worship hour griping about boring hymns.

It doesn't much matter what kind of instruments the worship team is using, or where the words are, if you have something to express from the heart. You just want to praise God. But if you have nothing to say, then all these details become extremely important and you conclude there's only one way to worship.

To have nothing inside to declare causes you to lose perspective, forcing you to cling desperately to routine and ritual: the way it's always been done. Churches decimated by back-stabbing, criticism, and factions focus on such commandments as "Special music shall always come after the pastoral prayer."

In contrast to the religion of pettiness, Jesus gives us an interesting picture of His kingdom. "The kingdom of heaven is like a mustard seed, which a man took and planted in his field. Though it is the smallest of all your seeds, yet when it grows, it is the largest of garden plants and becomes a tree, so that the birds of the air come and perch in its branches" (Matt. 13:31, 32).

The mustard seed religion Christ recommended always expands our lives. It is yeast working through the whole loaf of bread. The tiniest of seeds, it grows into a great tree that gives shade and shelter. The more we concentrate on God's positive qualities—for example, love, joy, and peace—the more expansive our religious life becomes. But the less we dwell on such essentials, the more our religion constricts around little details.

God doesn't want our religion to shrink us. He wants to expand our lives with His positive qualities, to nurture that good tree spreading its branches against the sky. Fill your minds, He says, "with whatever is true, whatever is noble, . . . whatever is admirable—if anything is excellent or praiseworthy— think about such things" (Phil. 4:8).

Don't just curse the darkness. "Live as children of light (for the fruit of the light consists in all goodness, righteousness and truth)" (Eph. 5:8, 9). It's a big world out there, with room to stretch out all kinds of branches and grow all kinds of fruit. "If anyone is in Christ, he is a new creation" (2 Cor. 5:17). Mustard seed religion is designed to help us grow into "the whole measure of the fullness of Christ" (Eph. 4:13).

There's such a lot to say about God, so many wonderful things we can express in our lives. We need to get beyond the religion of pettiness. As spiritual qualities deepen our heart, we'll notice less and less the broken candles on the edge of the sepulchre, and more and more the meaning of the Resurrection they witness to.

A FATE WORSE THAN DEATH

In the 1860s leprosy reached epidemic proportions among the natives of the Hawaiian islands. They had no natural immunity to it or to many other diseases brought by Whites in their trading vessels. The very survival of the Hawaiian people seemed threatened. As a result, the government passed and began strictly enforcing a segregation law. All confirmed cases of leprosy must leave society and remain in complete isolation. The authorities chose Kalawao, a stony but verdant promontory on the island of Molokai, as the isolation site. It was enclosed by a massive cliff that no one in poor health could climb, and the pounding surf of a rocky coastline.

Many Hawaiians regarded the law as inhumane. They distrusted the ability of White medical authorities to prescribe treatment for Hawaiian bodies. And they began calling the board of health the "board of death." White officials complained that the Hawaiians continued to eat, drink, and sleep with leprous relatives and hide them from those who "strive to root out the evil thing."

For the Hawaiian, something could be worse than death: to be forever cut off from a loved one. Not as appalled by the disfiguring illness as their White contemporaries, they still wanted to touch the afflicted relative. Whatever the consequences, he or she must not be driven out from the group. All Hawaiians needed to physically affirm and reaffirm their share in a common humanity. They needed to touch. Without that minimal sense of intimacy, life just wasn't worth living.

The islands faced a dilemma—segregation of the diseased violated the deepest fabric of Hawaiian culture, yet that segregation seemed the only way Hawaiian culture could itself survive. It was a dilemma Christian missionaries wrestled with a great deal. Such a profound moral question required thorough reflection. Forty-eight ministers gathered at an annual meeting and talked about it. They considered all the factors involved, carefully weighed all the pros and cons, and came up with what they considered a correct answer.

The missionaries' leaders decided to take a stand on which was the greater evil. They pronounced the leprosy plague "a loathsome, incurable, deadly disease fastening itself upon the 'vitals' of the nation," which in a few years could mean "the disorganization and total destruction of civilization, property values, and industry, of our churches, our contributions, our Hawaiian board and its work of missions."

They also issued a statement about what sort of action the government should take. "While striving to comfort and strengthen with the love of Jesus the afflicted hearts of the lepers and their friends," we must "teach and persuade all the people to obey the law of God and segregate the lepers from among us," and "teach every leper who cleaves to his people and refuses to go away, that he is sinning against the lives of men and against the law of God."

In the 1860s, 48 sincere people arrived at a credible choice of the lesser of two evils. While it would cause heartrending partings at the docks in Honolulu, at least it would prevent the destruction of a whole population.

The missionaries in Hawaii came up with a reasonable response to the leprosy crisis. But we can't help feeling, "There's got to be more to it than that."

It would take a Belgian farm boy named Joseph Damien de Veuster to show just exactly what that "something more" is.

THE POWER OF TOUCH

Joseph had an enormous appetite for serving God. At the age of 20 he entered holy orders. Prostrated before an altar, priests covered him with a black mortuary pall, sprinkled him with holy water, then raised him up to poverty, chastity, and obedience with the Congregation of the Sacred Heart. Joseph thrived in an environment of radical consecration. During his training the words of Christ, "Go teach all nations," impressed him deeply, and he developed a passion for missionary service.

His superiors doubted his abilities at first, not believing he could manage the ecclesiastical studies one had to pursue in order to become a priest. But Joseph surprised them, poring stubbornly over Latin texts hour after hour until he could decipher them and pass the necessary tests. He still didn't have the intellectual equipment to balance a variety of moral factors and come up with the correct sum. What he did have was a passion to echo Christ, to live as He did.

Joseph, now called Father Damien, finally got his chance to go and teach. His order sent him to the Hawaiian islands and assigned the young man a district on the island of Hawaii, where the population was scattered over a thousand square miles of volcanic peaks and steep slopes. It took him six weeks of strenuous hiking just to get around to his parishioners. Most men would have collapsed after a few months, but Father Damien found a congenial challenge in a physically demanding life. Carrying candles, sacraments, and a portable altar on his back over rugged terrain, he called the faithful with a conch shell. He became an accomplished builder of chapels. When felling trees in the highlands or hauling up shipped-in logs from the beach, he enjoyed carrying the heaviest beams himself.

After several years of ministry he confronted that thorny problem of leprosy, segregation, and the settlement on Molokai. And he arrived at a very different answer. It was Easter, and Father Damien was 33. He deliberately crossed from the world of the well to the world of the mortally ill, choosing to minister to and live with the people at the Kalawao settlement. It was a simple matter, in a way. The lepers needed a priest; Damien volunteered and went on a temporary basis, but then found the work of his life.

The man was not an aging or sickly saint who had decided to spend his remaining years in heroic service, but a robust, active priest described by contemporaries as a man "in the prime of life . . . and the perfection of youthful health and vigor." He did not come to the island blindly. "You know my disposition," he told superiors. "I want to sacrifice myself for the poor lepers." But neither was he a morbid holy man looking for martyrdom. "I am not yet a leper," he wrote his brother, "and with the miraculous help of God . . . I hope I never will be."

Father Damien arrived on Molokai with little more than a breviary. But he quickly built himself a shack, began visiting the people in their huts, and started services in which he addressed the congregation not as "my brothers," but as "we lepers." Damien touched the people physically as well as spiritually, and won many converts.

A doctor once assigned there had the habit of setting his medicines on his gatepost so the afflicted could receive his help—from a distance. They did not want it. Another doctor who made rounds at the settlement hospital conducted physical examinations by raising the rags on a diseased body with his cane. A minister who had visited preached the good word—from the elevated and safe distance of a veranda.

The men were being quite reasonable and correct, of course. If segregation was necessary, then self-segregation also must be practiced. One had no right to take any taint of the disease back to the land of the living.

But Damien was not a visitor. Entering squalid huts, he cleaned and bandaged open sores, applied salves and ointments, and prescribed pills. He also labored for conversions. "Here I give words of sweetness and consolation; there, I mix in a little bitterness, because it is necessary to open the eyes of a sinner."

Damien ministered willingly, but he was not a plastic saint impervious to the physical horrors around him. He wrote to friends of the fetid odor arising constantly from toes and fingers being eaten away. The smell of the congregation at his church was so bad that at Communion time he feared he wouldn't be able to swallow the consecrated wine. "Sometimes, confessing the sick," he wrote, "whose sores are full of worms like cadavers in the grave, I have to hold my nose." But Damien would not turn away. He stuck it out in the confessional and struggled to overcome overwhelming nausea and headaches that lasted for days.

He also started smoking a pipe to disguise the odors that clung to his clothes, and had someone send a pair of heavy boots to protect his legs from the "peculiar itching which I usually experience every evening after my visiting." Damien stayed and continued to touch, continued to say "we lepers," and in time no longer had to force himself. He lived and worked cheerfully, and ate with a good appetite.

The priest had plenty of work to do. The Hawaiians there had a saying: "In this place there is no law." After all, what legal punishments could threaten those already imprisoned for life, awaiting an unpleasant death? And so the weak huddled in dark houses, wrapped in filthy bedclothes, hoping that somehow they could crawl out to the boat that brought shipments of food and get their fair share. The strong, grown accustomed to taking from others whatever they desired, seemed "to want for nothing from soft slippers to hair oil."

Children suffered the most, especially those whose parents had died or simply abandoned them. The unscrupulous sometimes used them as drudges or child prostitutes, then simply threw them out when they became too deformed by the disease.

Surrounded by such tragedies, Damien pled and preached and sometimes threatened. He would invade a dance place known as the "crazy pen," where drunken men and women mingled, and break up the festivities with moral outrage and a walking stick.

He also began taking orphans under his wing, building dormitories and kitchens for them near his presbytery. Slowly Damien created beauty amid a harsh, forbidding landscape of the dying. Fashioning flutes out of old coal-oil cans, which the lepers managed to play with only two or three fingers, he gave them the gift of music. Damien took great pains to ensure that charity did not come in anonymous bulk, but that each man, woman, and child at the settlement received a gift package addressed individually to him or her.

Each Sunday young and old believers gathered at his church, St. Philomena's, the women in long-sleeved gowns and beribboned straw hats, the men in calico shirts and white trousers, all of them draped in flower leis. Together they sat quietly in the brightly painted interior, a poignant mixture of hope and decay. The candles were usually set at odd angles, the holy water font was a tin cup, and the decorations were rather tawdry, but the occasional visitor came away impressed by the beauty of the congregation's singing, the fervor of their prayers, the earnestness with which they brought their broken, doomed bodies forward to receive the sacraments.

On those occasions Kalawao became a community. It was no longer just a place where the dying fought for food and tried to forget their misery in drunkenness. Here was Christ's body, a living part of the whole. Here human beings could grow in the Spirit.

To build it, Damien had to endure years of isolation. He frequently begged his superiors to send another priest to work with him, but that was, understandably, a difficult assignment to fill. For more than half his time on Molokai he had no one, and he felt it keenly. "Being deprived of the companionship of my colleagues of our dear congregation," he wrote, "is more painful to bear than leprosy." Still the man stayed on.

Father Damien outlasted three complete population turnovers at Kalawao, but after 12 years of ministry there, his "we lepers" invocation became a physical reality. He lost all feeling in his left foot, and the telltale atrophy of the skin began to appear. Damien did not fall apart at his death sentence, but simply prayed that his Lord would grant him grace to carry his cross "on our peculiar Golgotha of Kalawao." He had taken the risk with eyes wide open. It was the price of touching.

Father Damien used his strength to the end, redoubling his efforts into what a biographer called "a kind of priestly perpetual motion." A visiting priest was astonished to find him on top of a church, putting on the roof, energetically directing masons and carpenters. The disease by now was grossly evident. His face was puffy, his ears swollen and elongated, his eyes red, and his voice hoarse. But Damien expressed thanks that his hands, though quite sore, were not yet crippled.

Unlike the men arguing the implications of the leper problem on property values and civilization, Damien did not solve an abstract problem—he expressed his passion. He was compelled to express something greater than himself.

What made Damien, among all those other believers standing on the sidelines, the one who showed the world "something more"? Why did he demonstrate what the kingdom was really like: a great tree spreading its branches against the sky, providing God's creatures with shade and shelter? It was surely the quality of his faith. He had moved far beyond the religion of pettiness and was seeking something much bigger—God Himself.

In fact, Father Damien experienced a remarkable intimacy with God on that isolated island. He developed the disciplined skill of being intimate, rising each day at 5:00 a.m. for "morning prayer—adoration and meditation until 6:30." The priest was highly conscious of where his inner resources came from. In his "personal rule" he admonished himself: "Unite your heart with God. . . . May passion lead you to whisper these words continually: 'I wish to be dissolved and to be with Christ.' "

A visitor at Kalawao, strolling with him by the shore one day, stopped to cool off and waded into the water. Looking back to the beach, he was impressed by the "quiet way" Damien "sat down and read and prayed while I bathed, retiring at once into that hidden life which was so real to him."

Father Damien wanted more than just a balanced perspective. It wasn't enough for him to have the right answers—he had to give himself away. And the reason he could do that so heroically was his humble walk with God.

The intimacy that all the great men and women of God have experienced down through the ages started with the apostles. Paul could say that all his former privileges were rubbish compared to the "surpassing greatness of knowing Christ Jesus my Lord" (Phil. 3:8). John could talk from experience about the great love that the Father lavishes on His children. Peter could testify that a relationship with Christ filled the believer "with an inexpressible and glorious joy" (1 Peter 1:8).

Here is the essence of healthy religion. It must deepen our hearts and lead us to intimacy with God. Without that connection, everything we do dissolves into pettiness. But with that connection, our world will expand immeasurably, and we'll find ourselves living as children of light, bearing much good fruit.